# Welcome

## To The

## Wild Horse

## Coloring Book

## For Girls

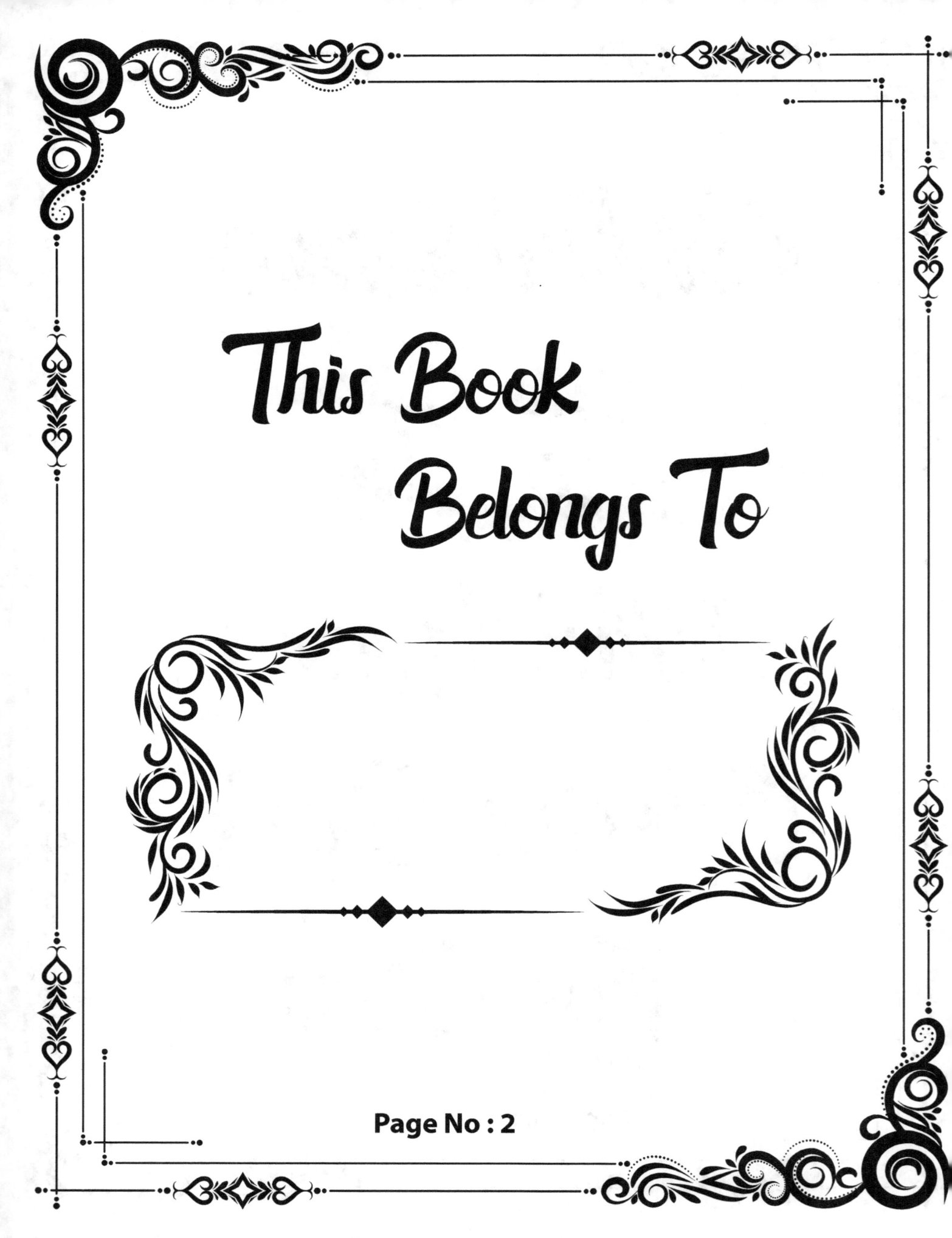

# This Book Belongs To

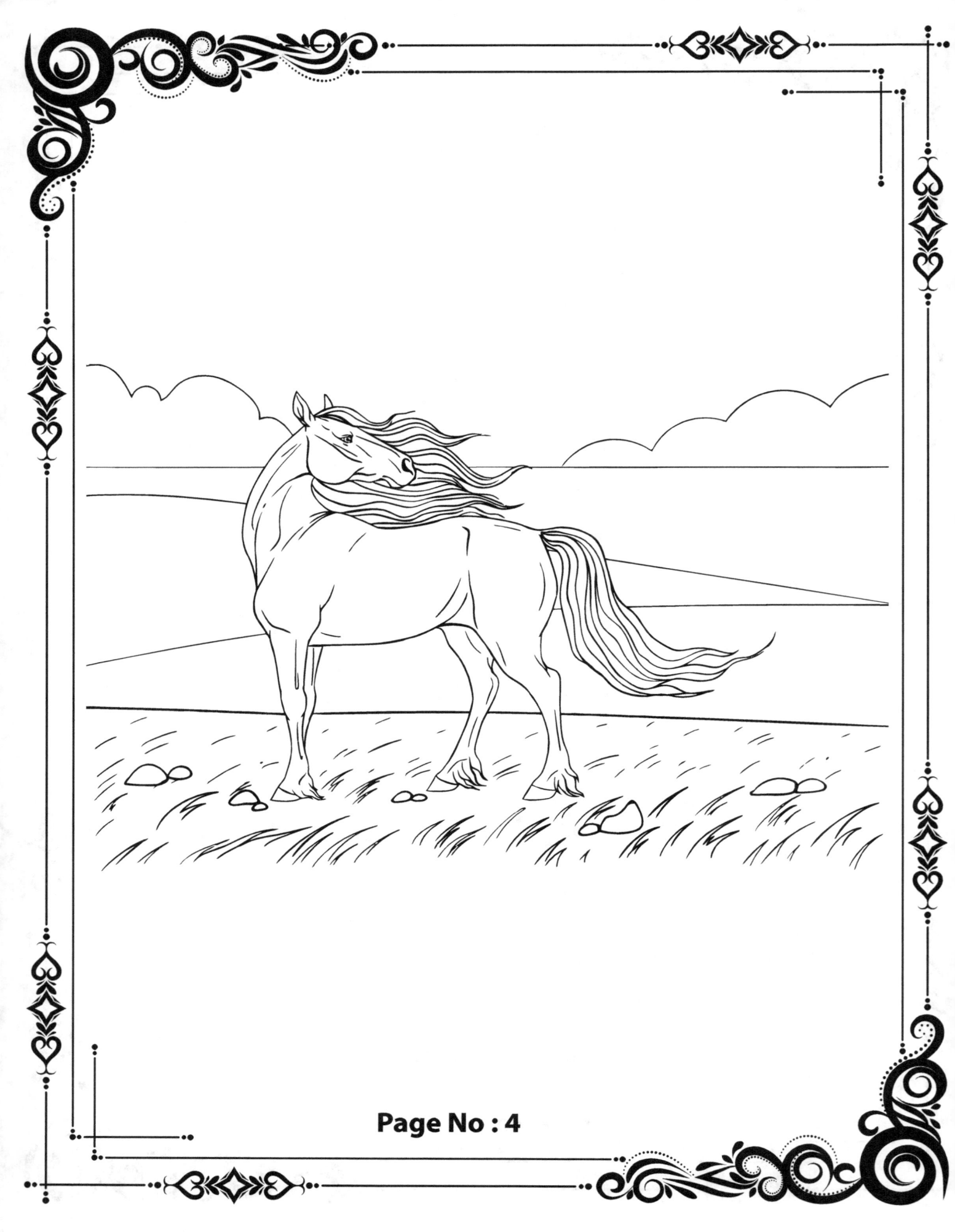

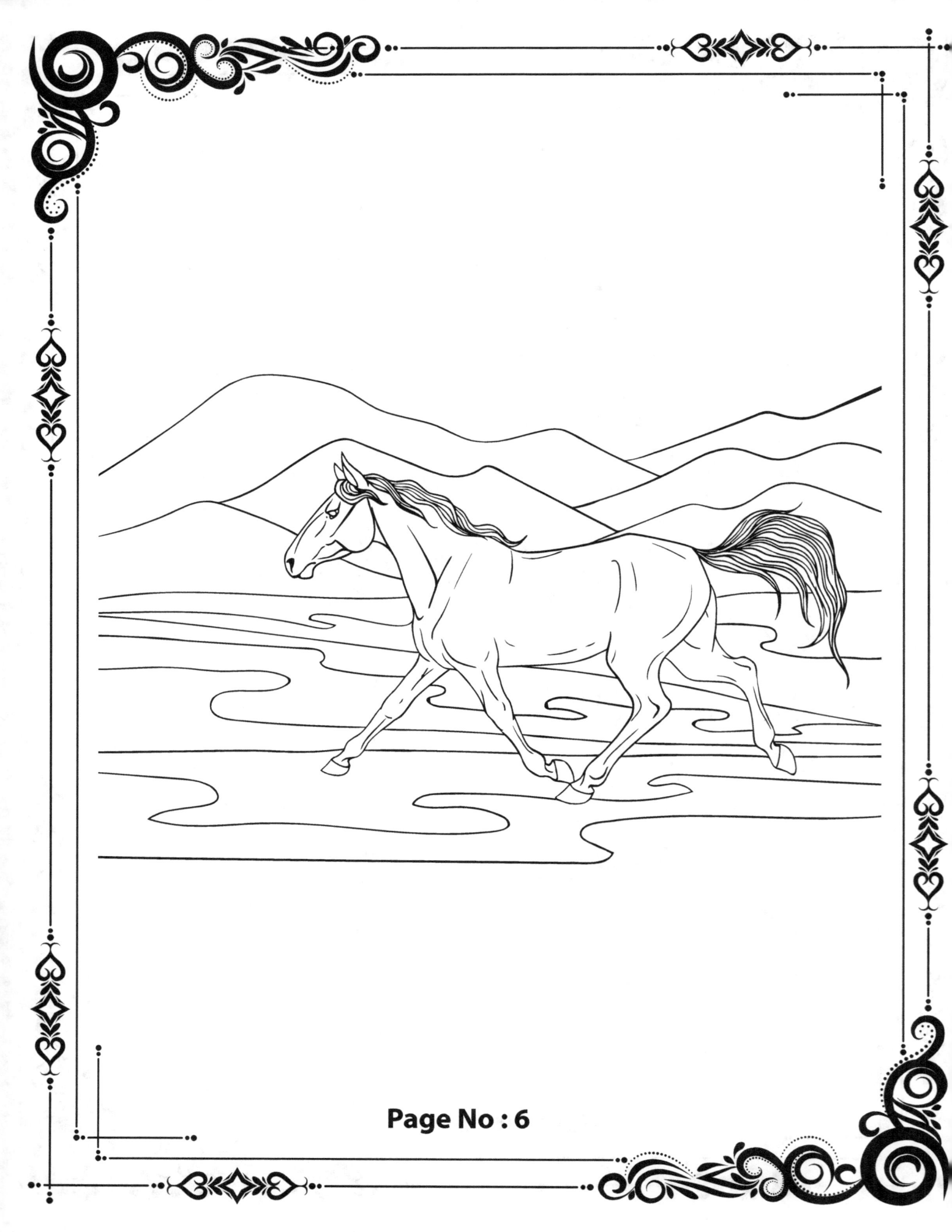

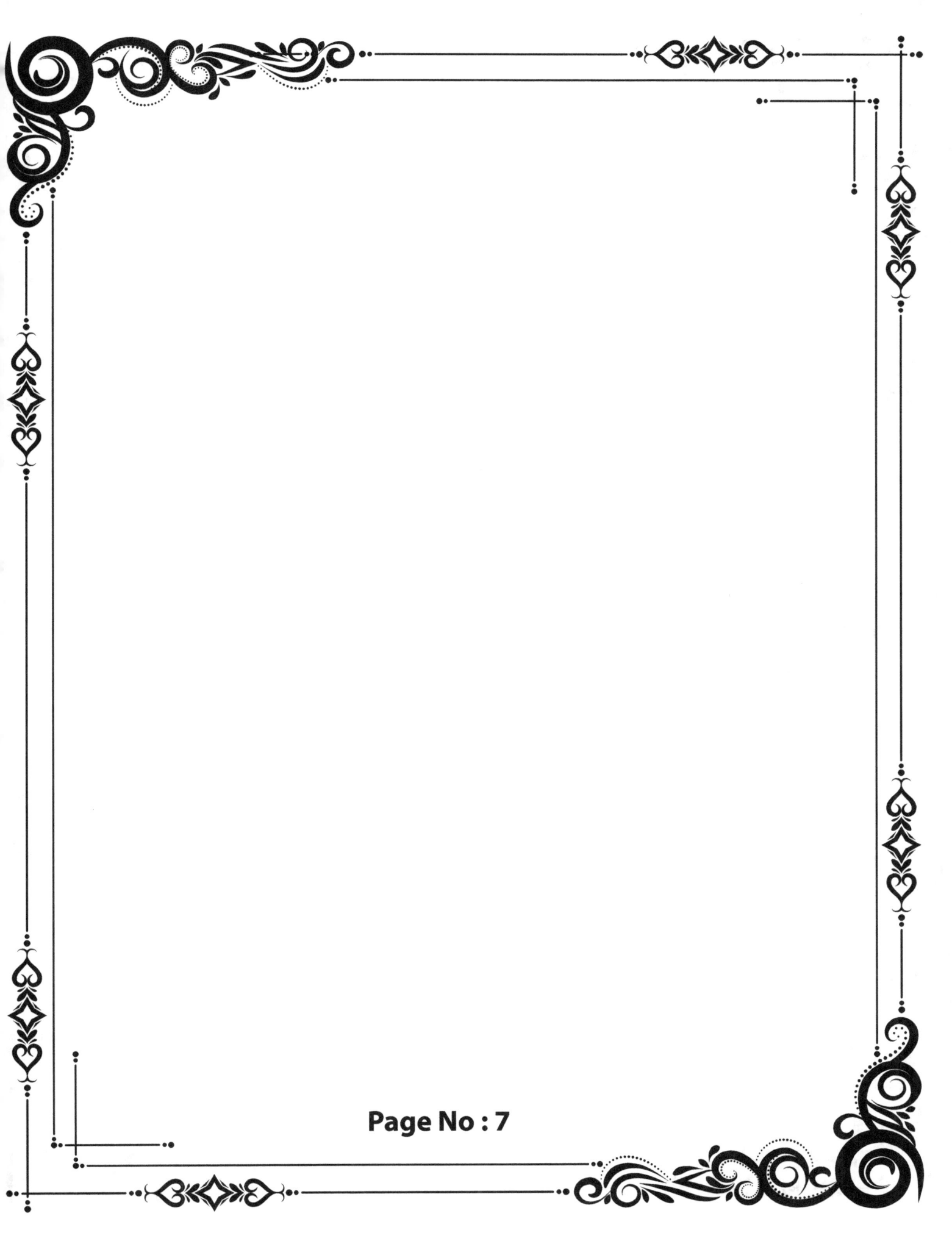

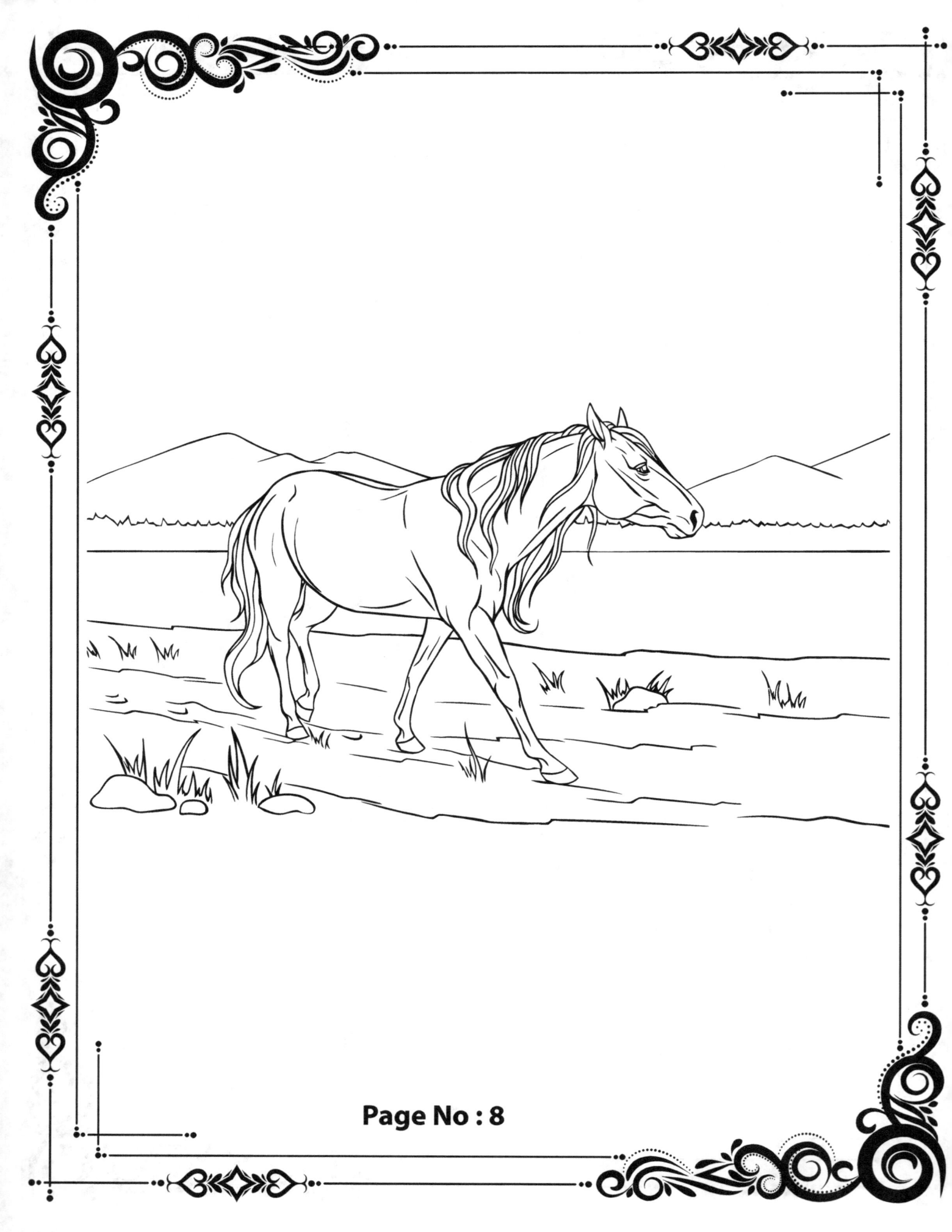

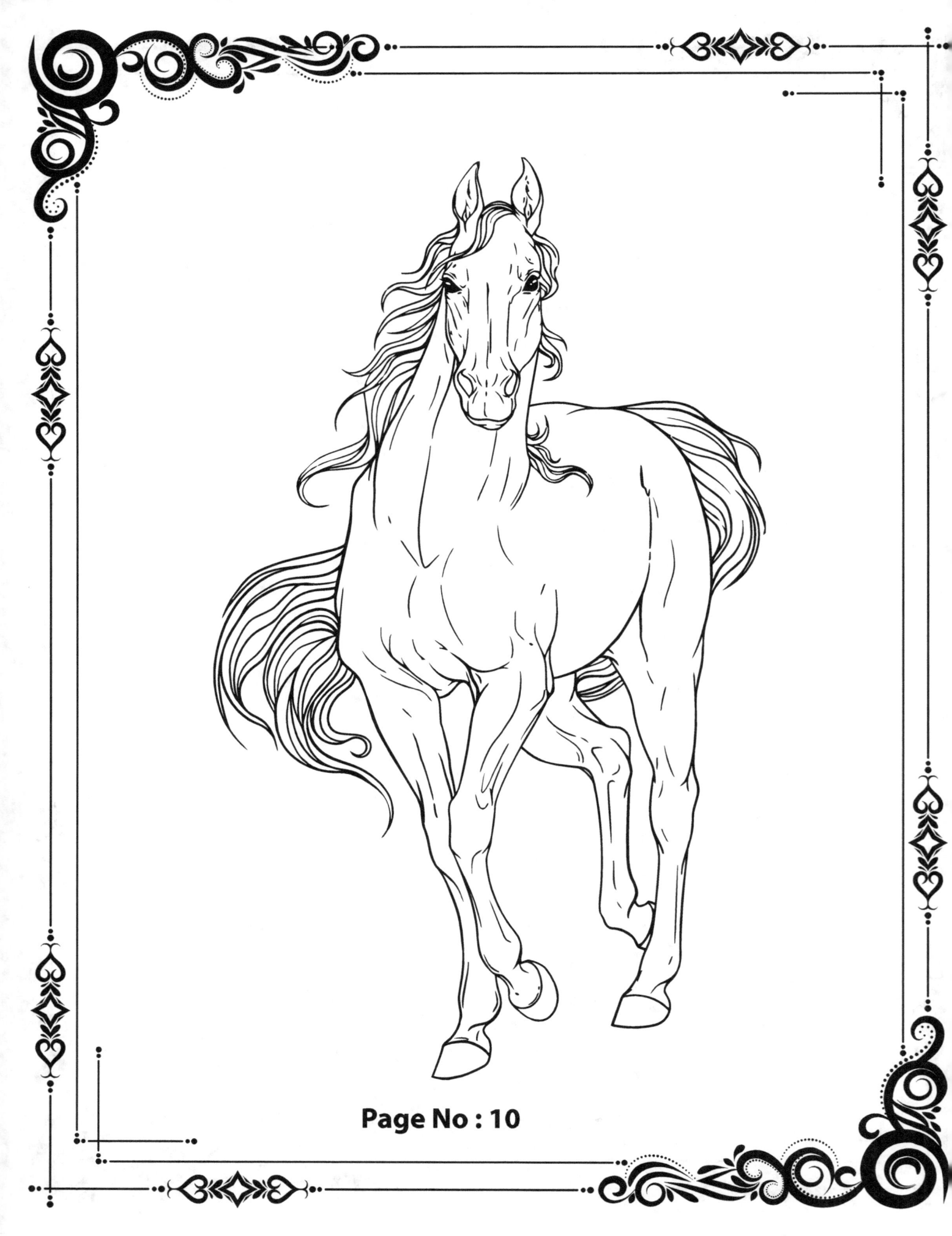

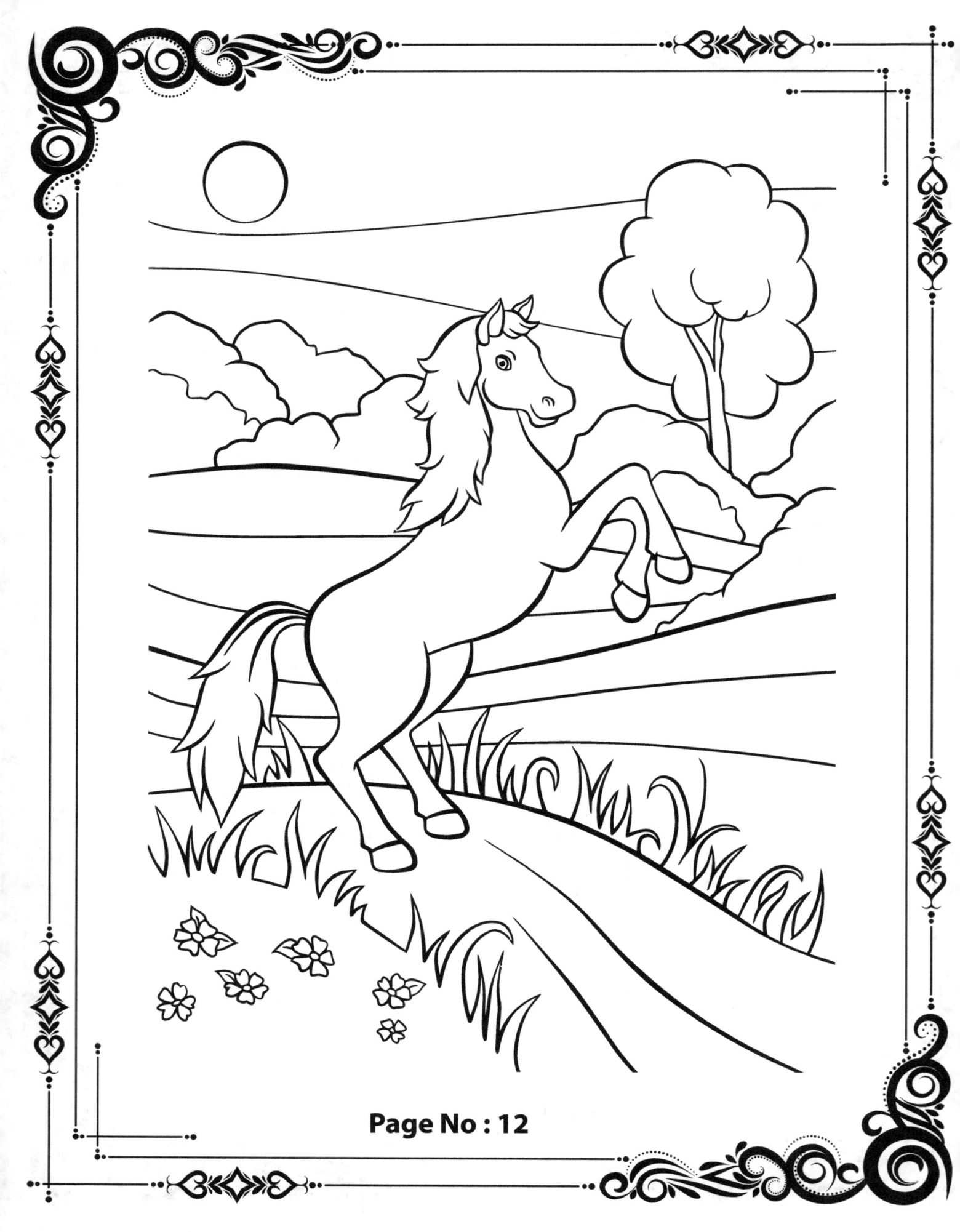

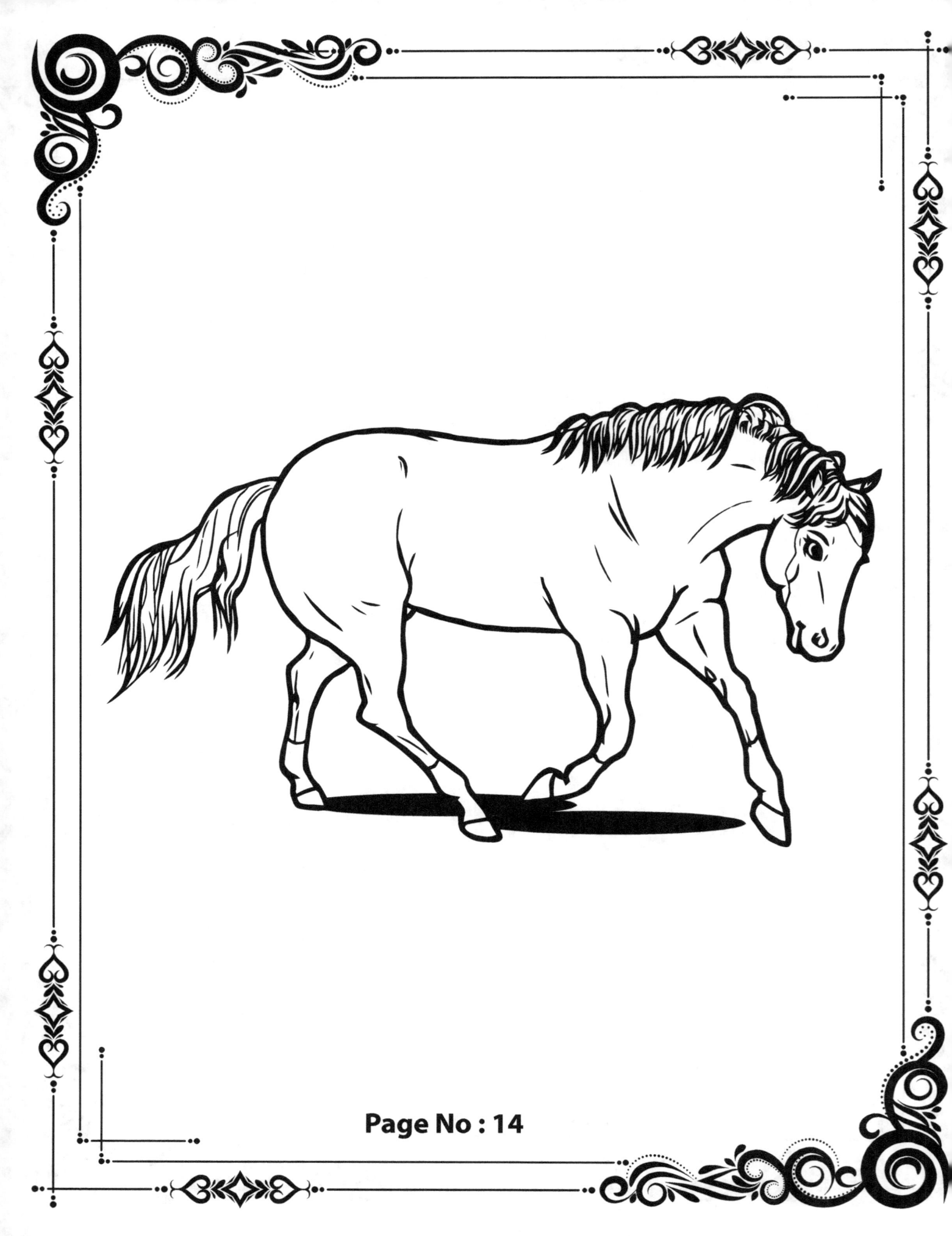

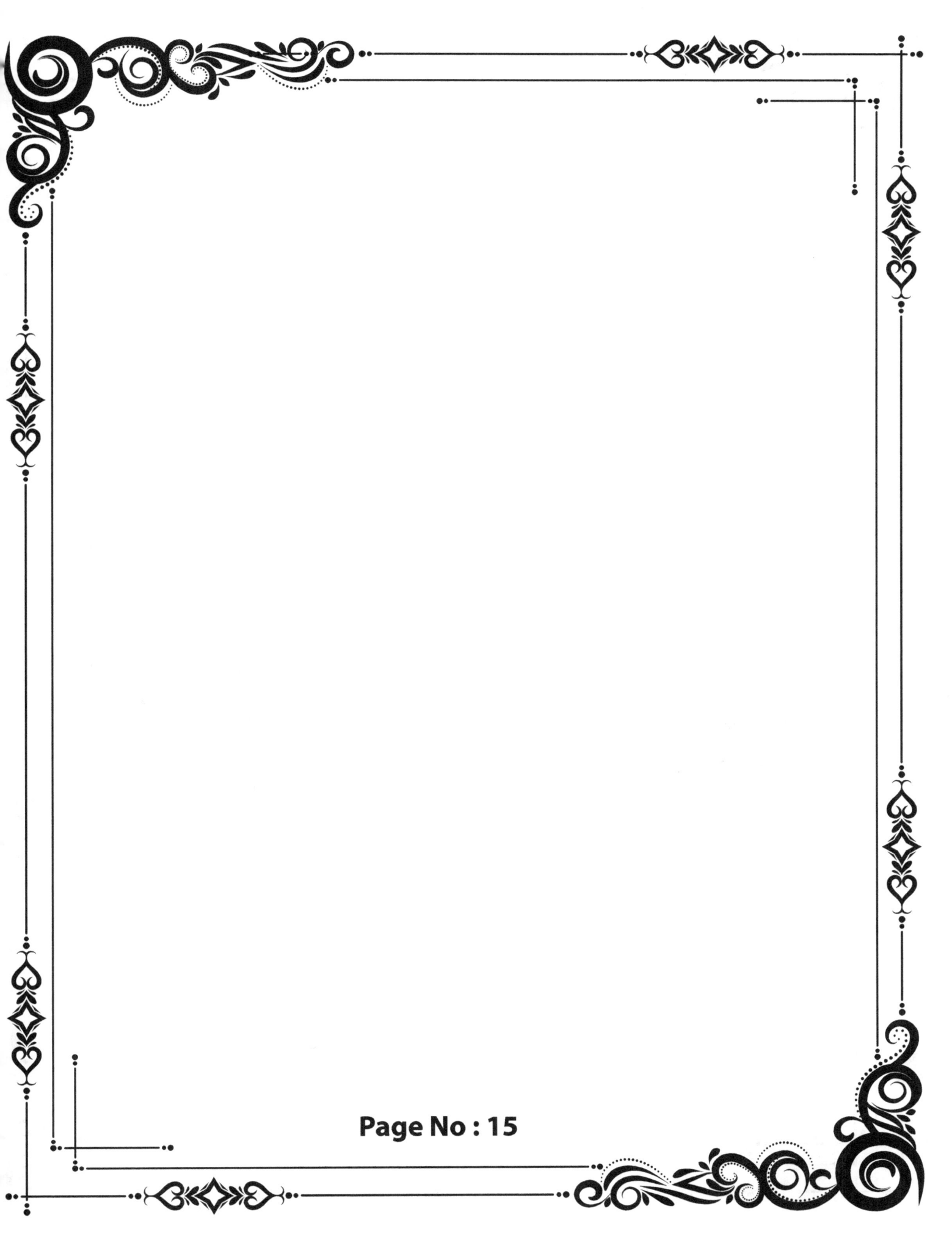

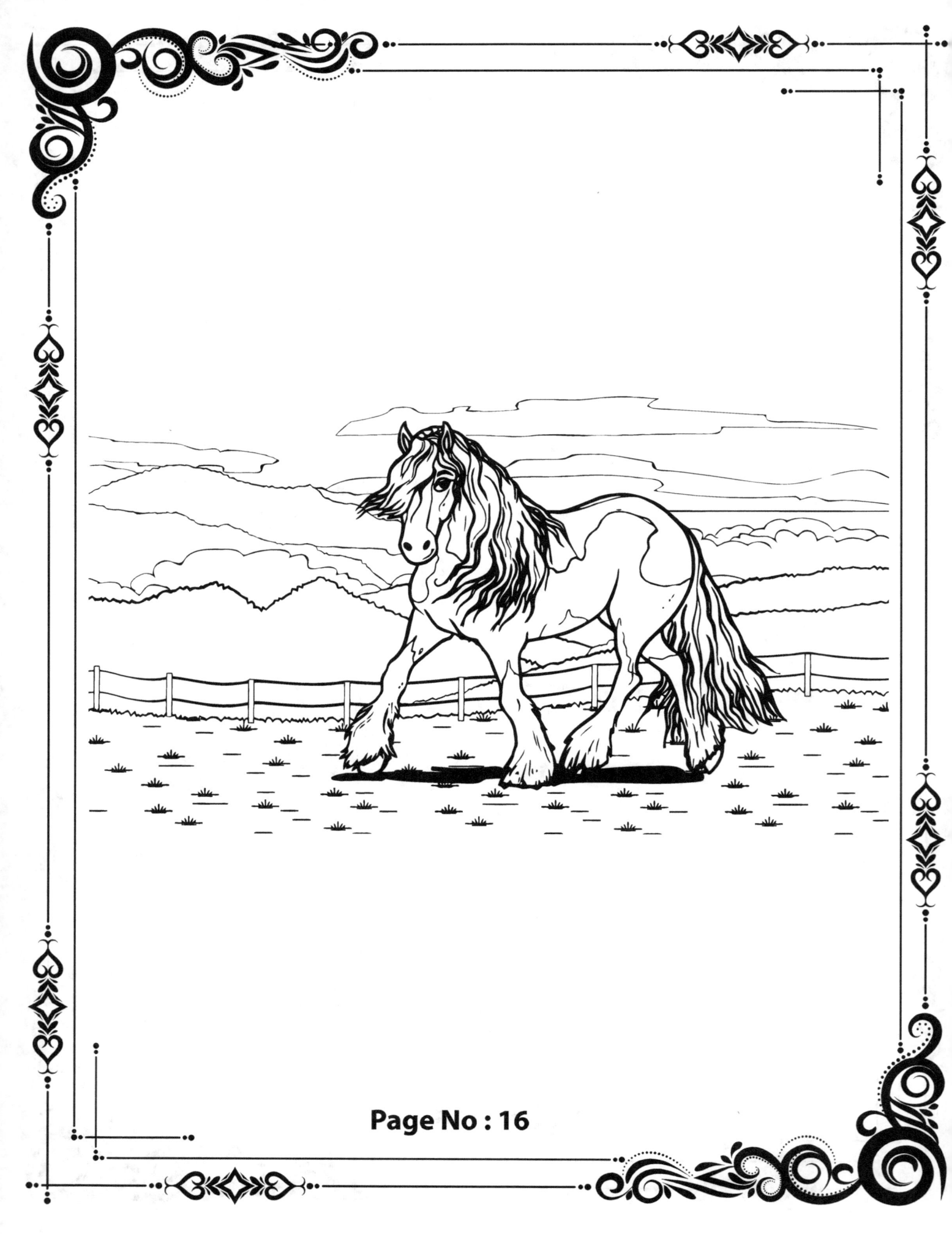

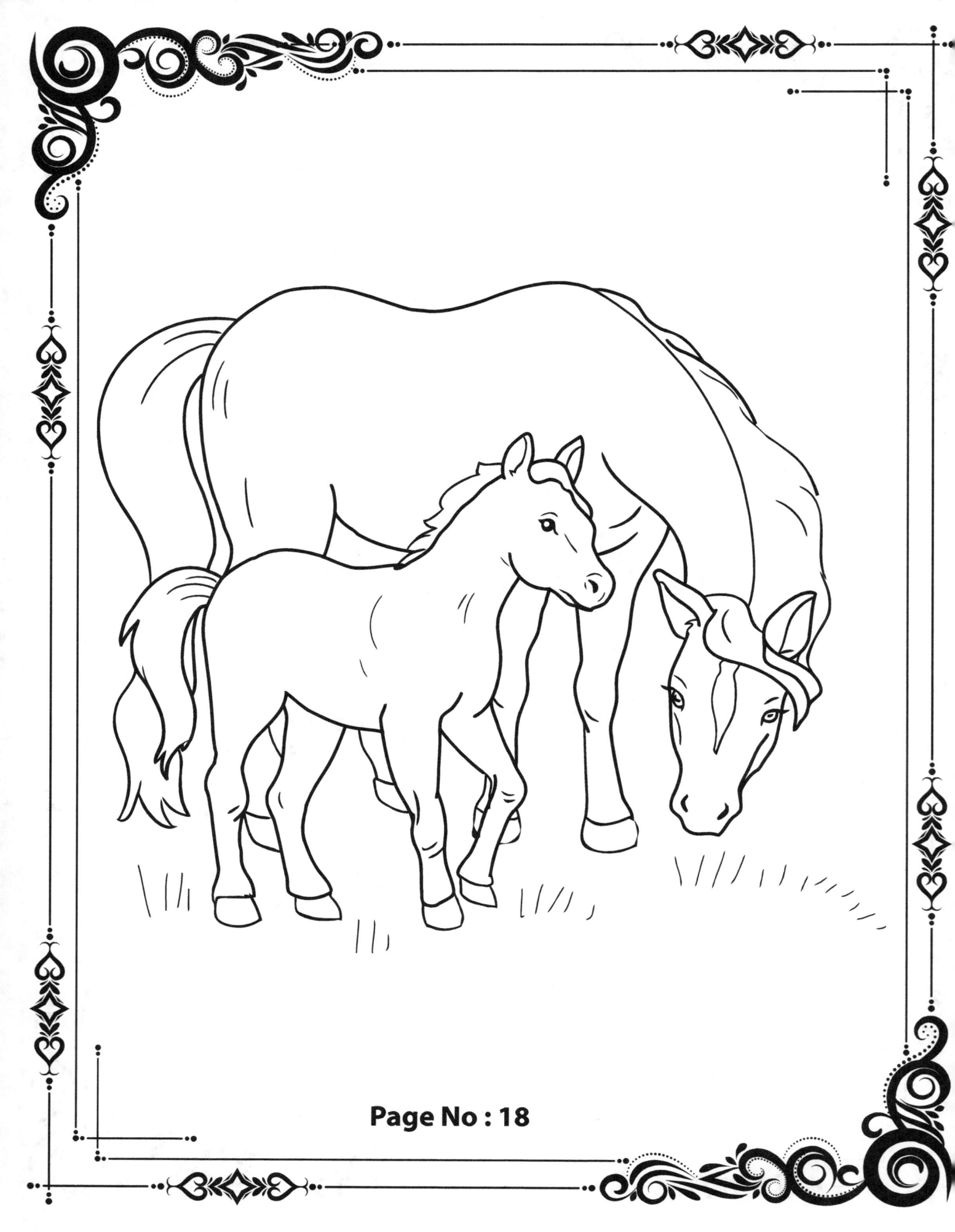

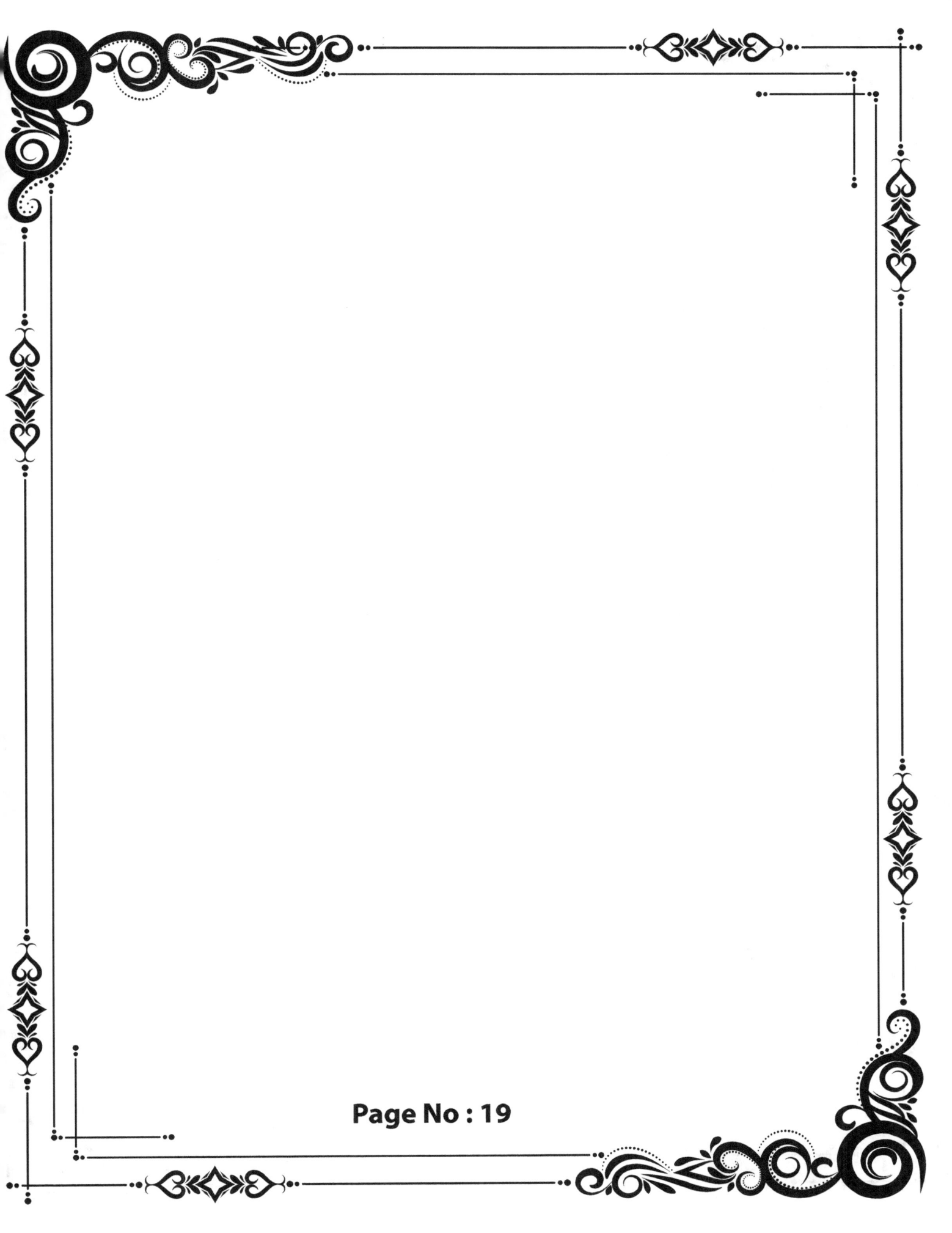

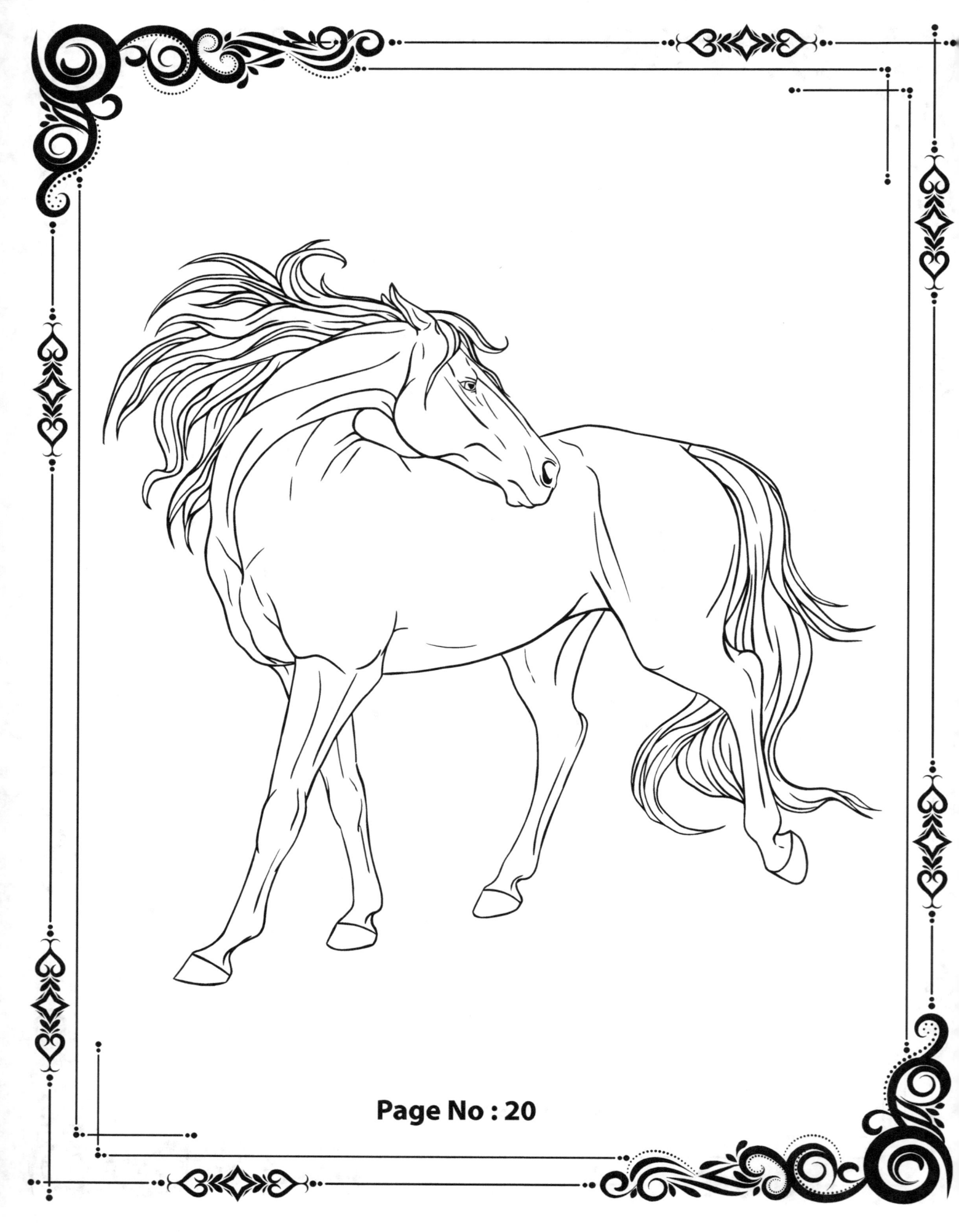

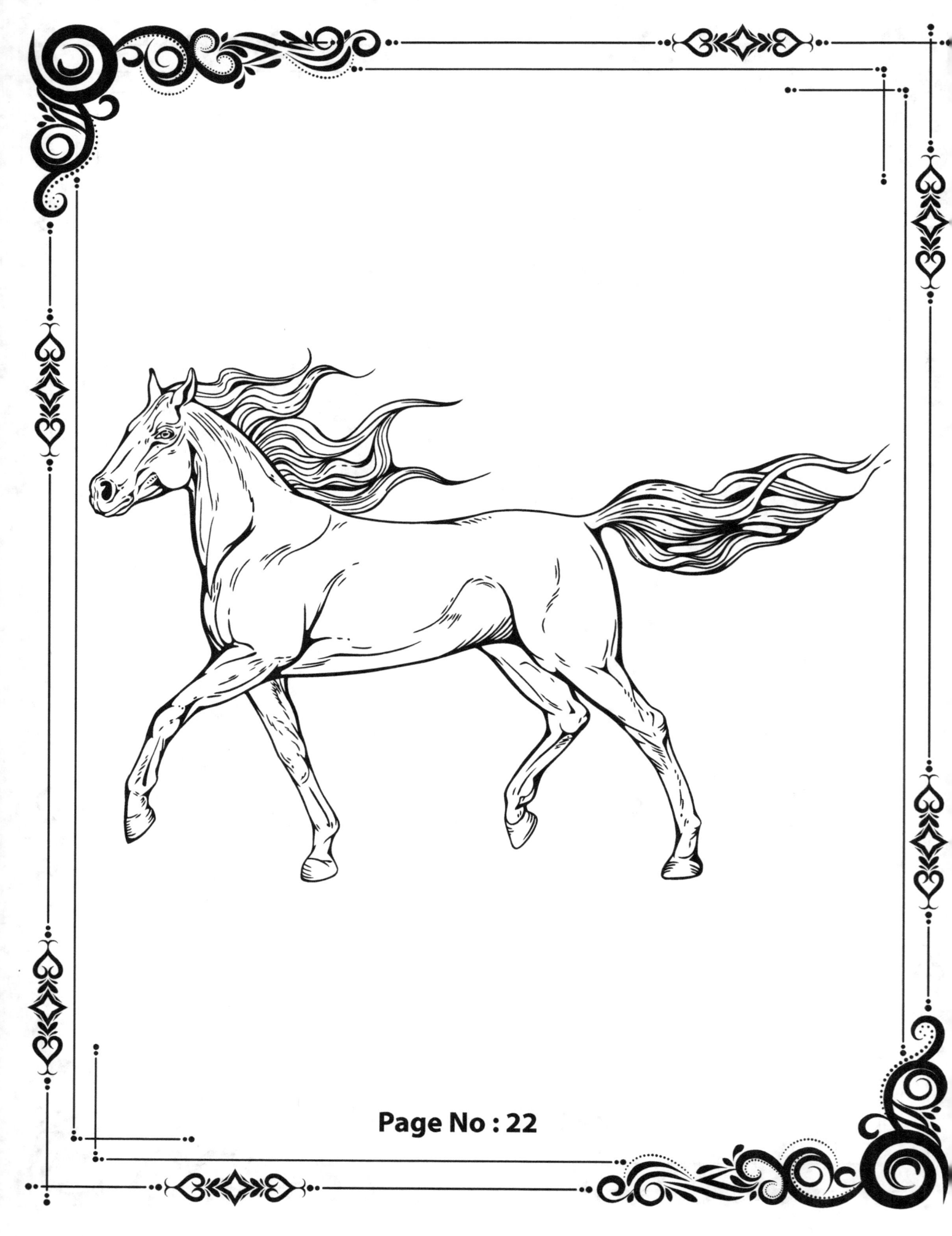

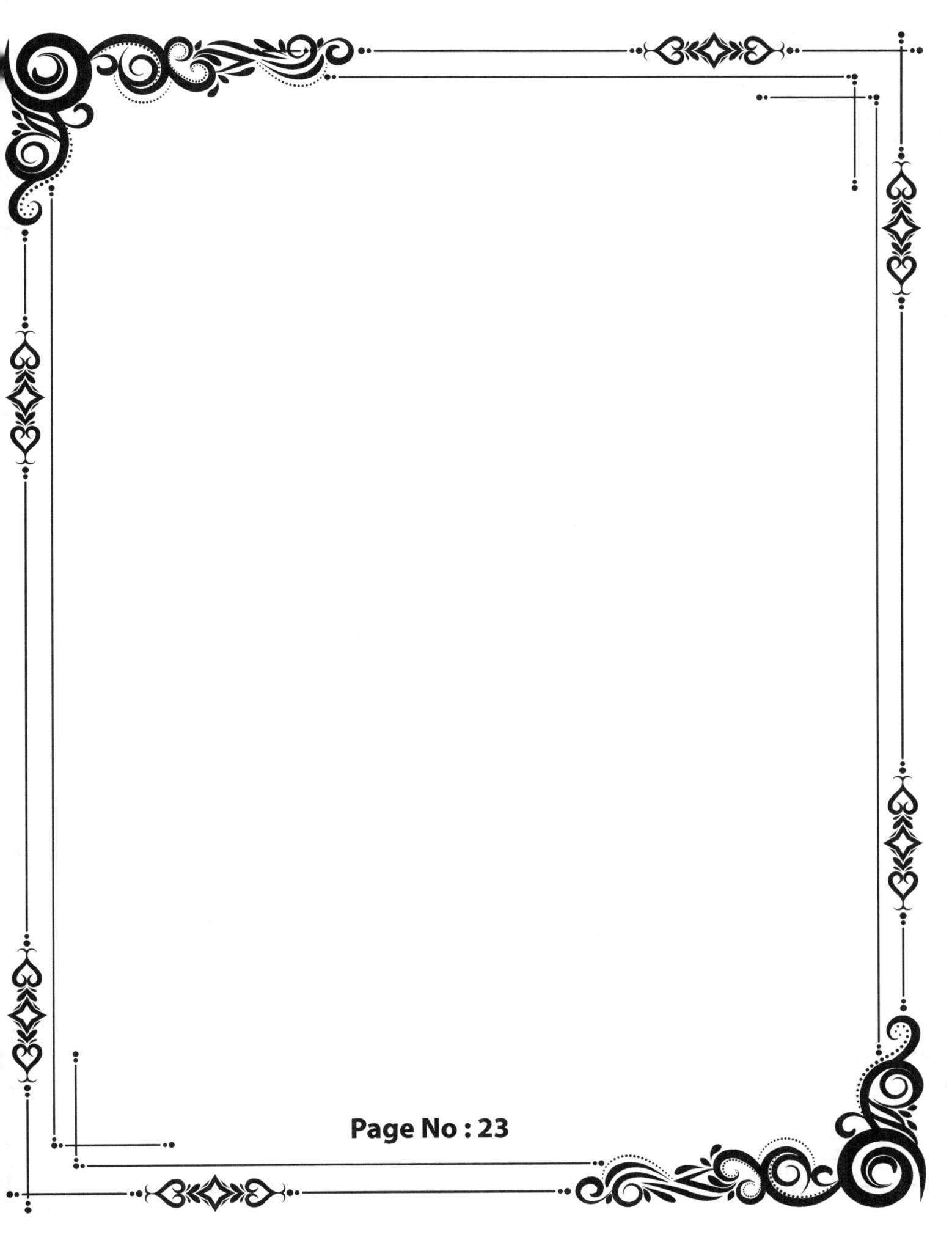

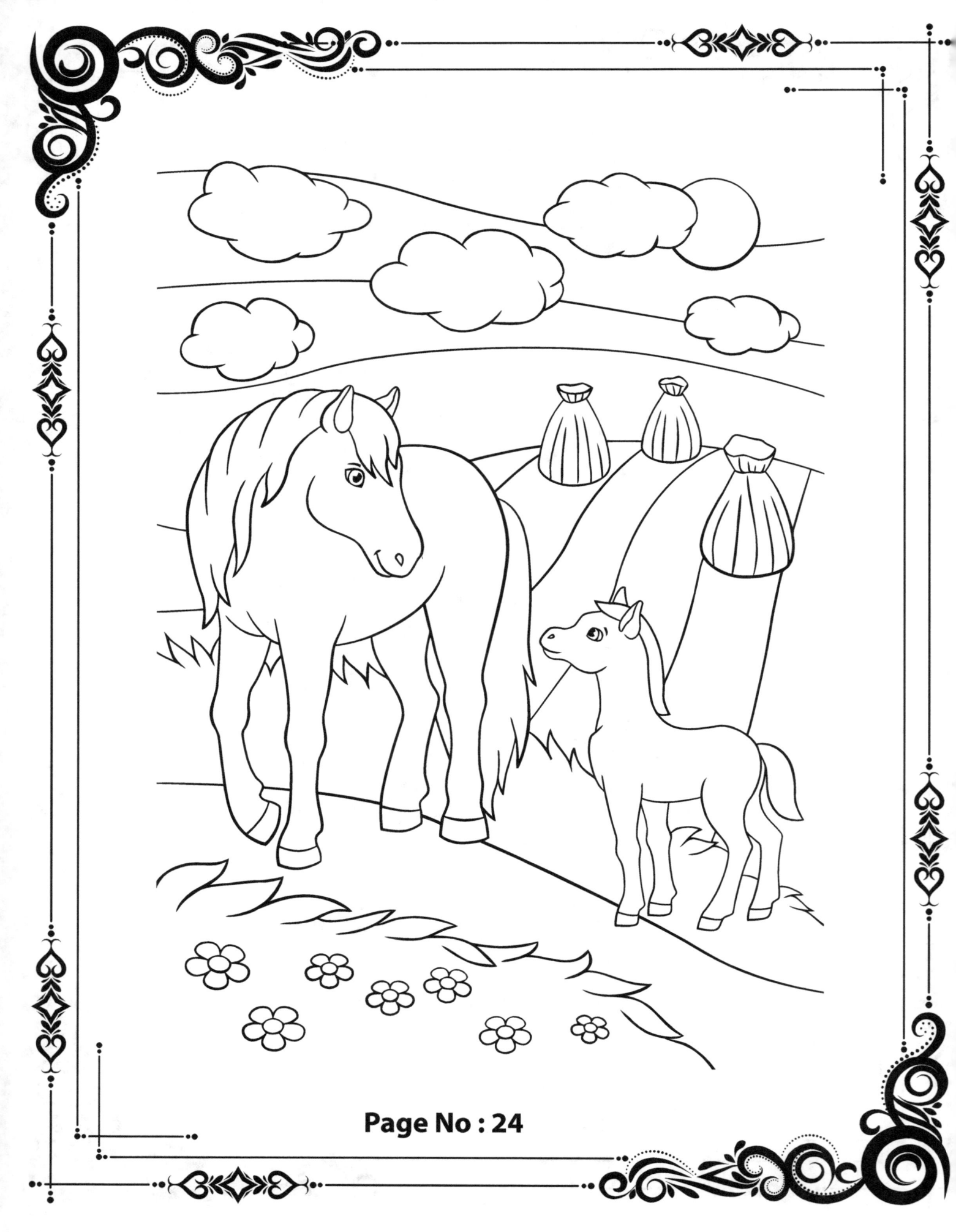

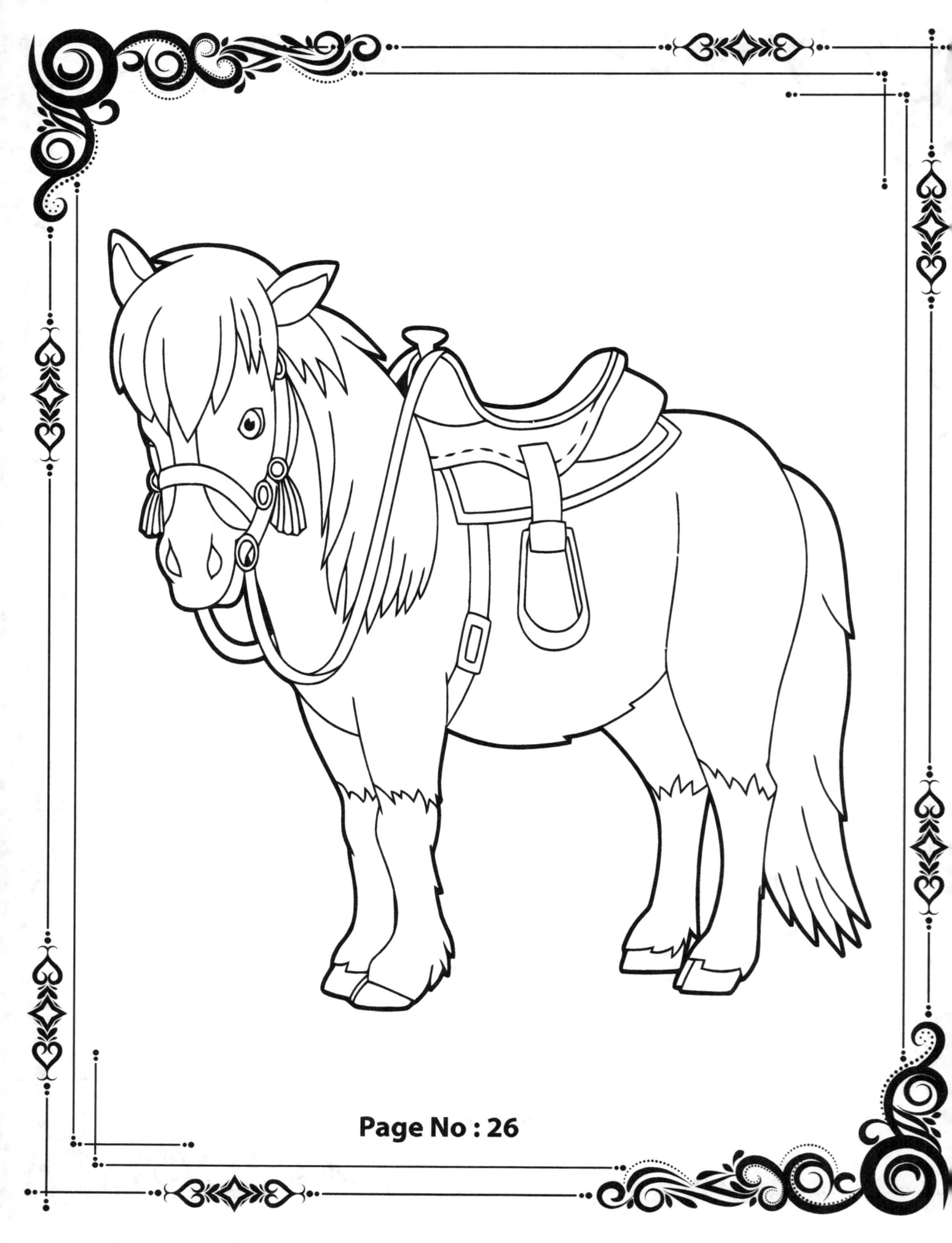

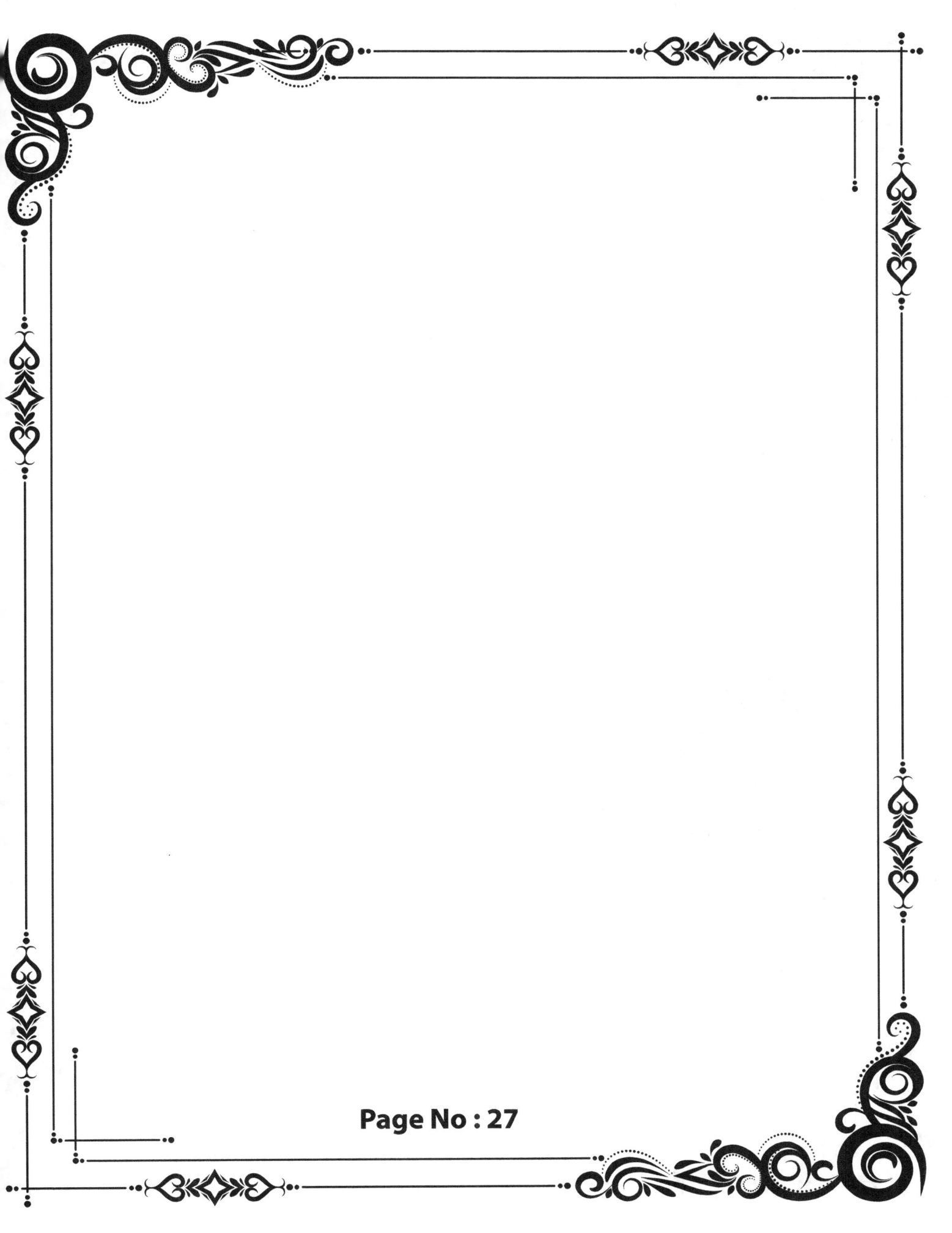

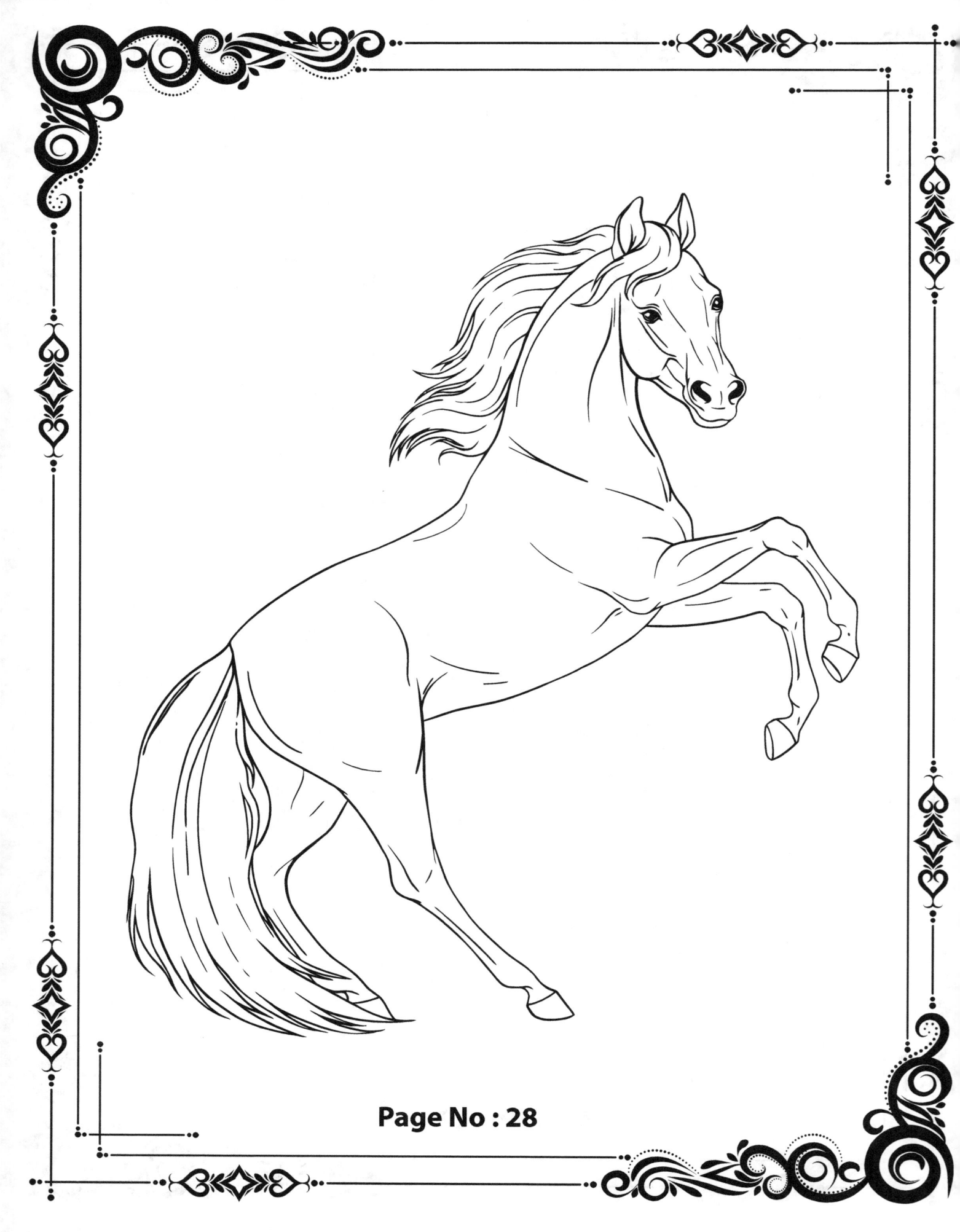

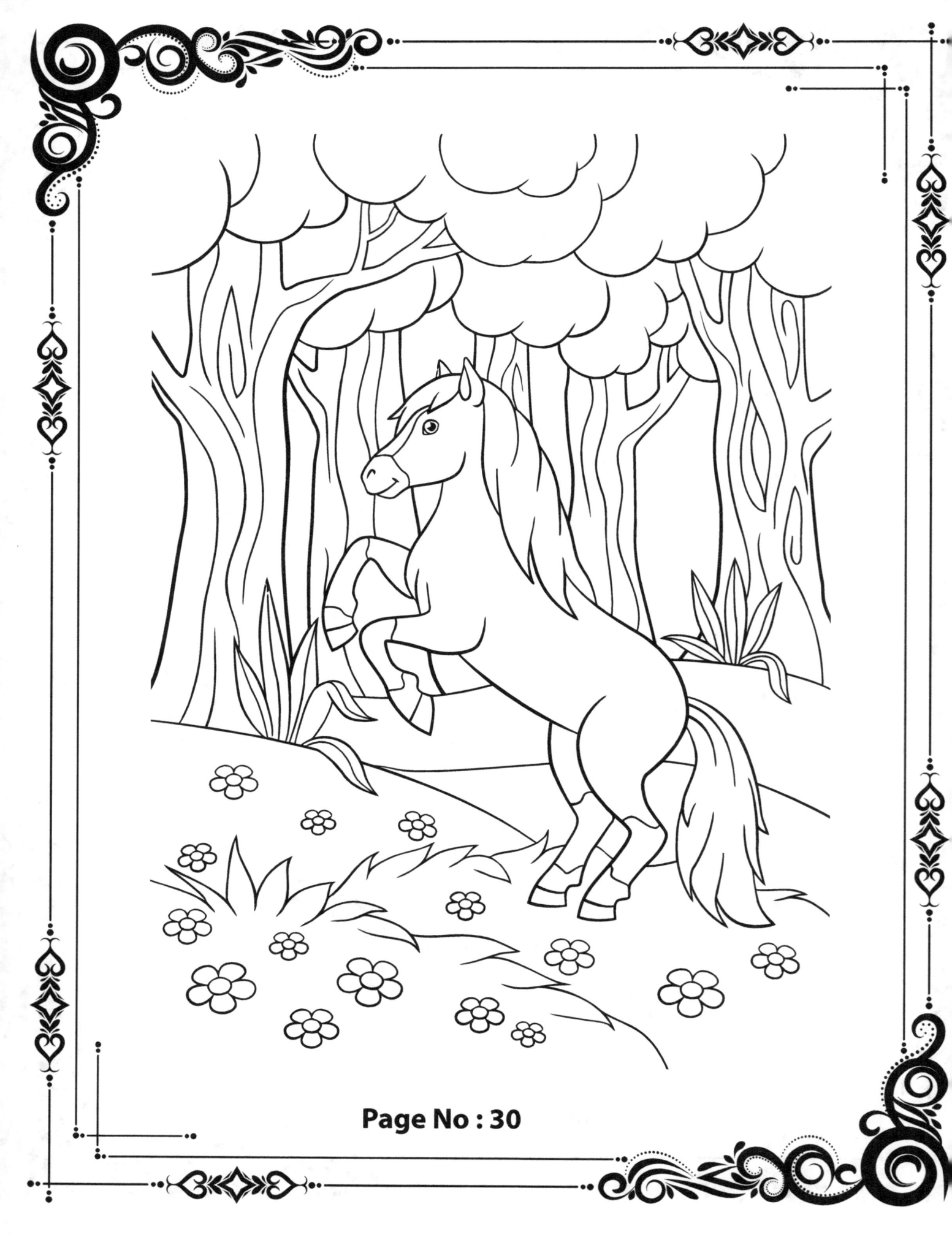

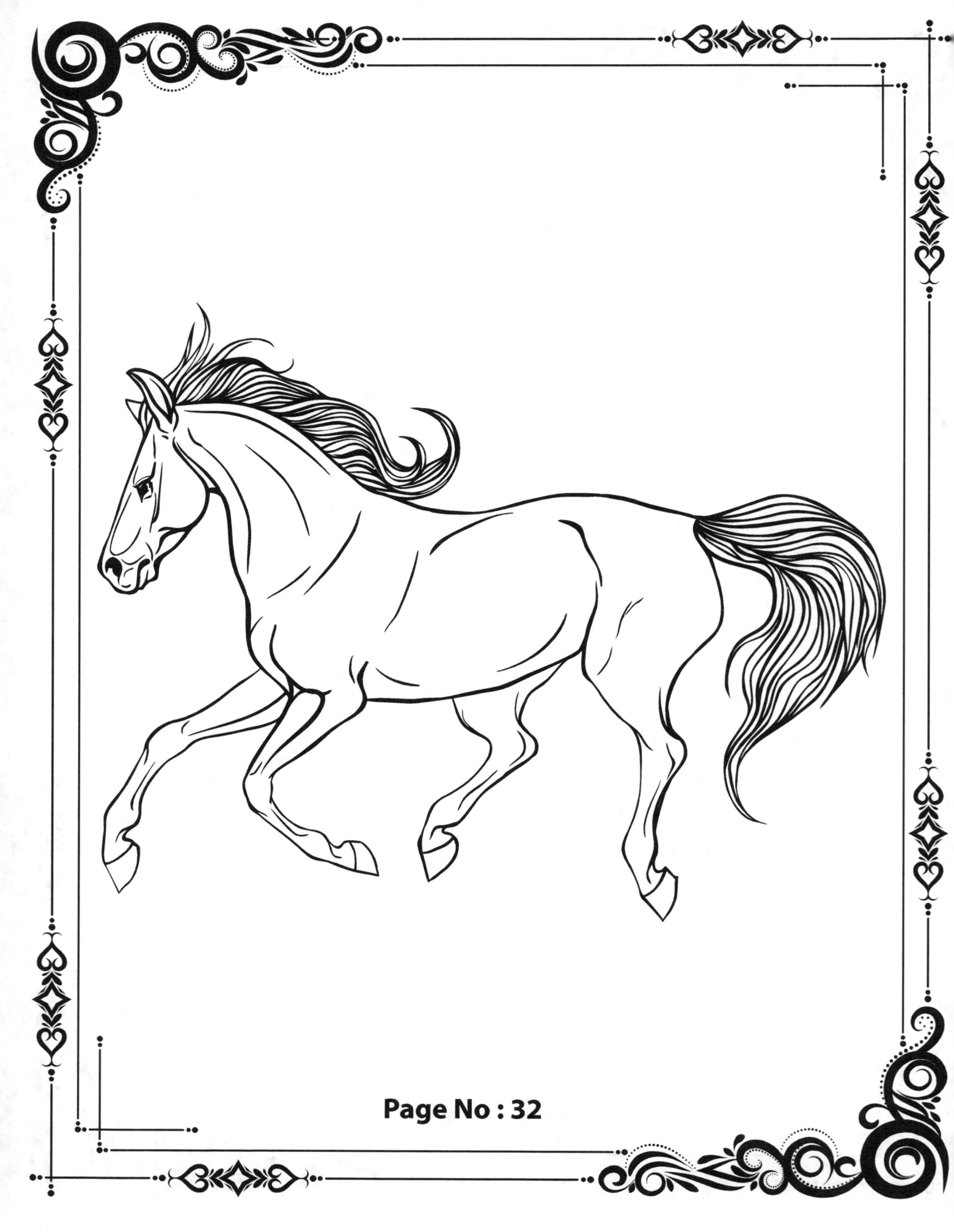

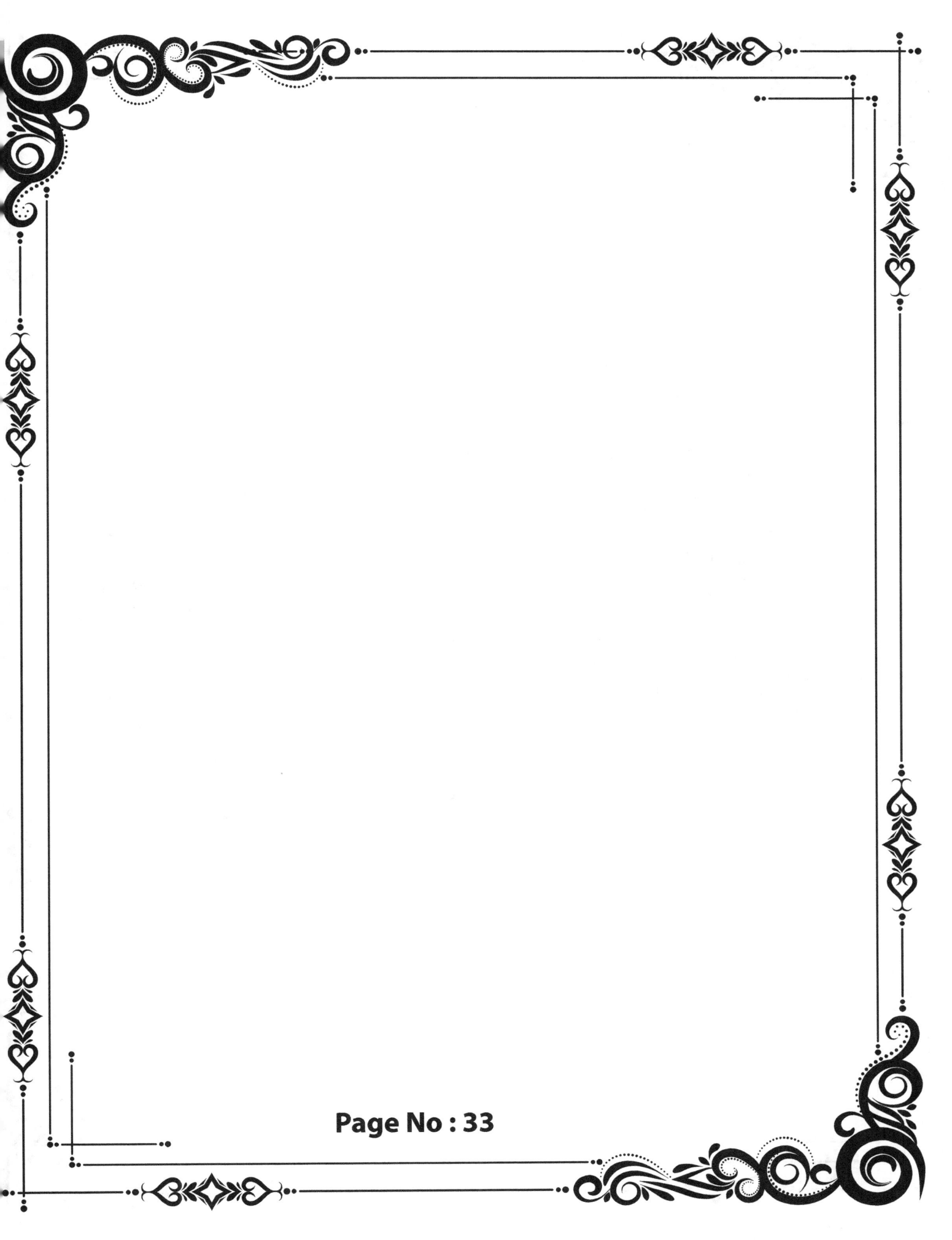

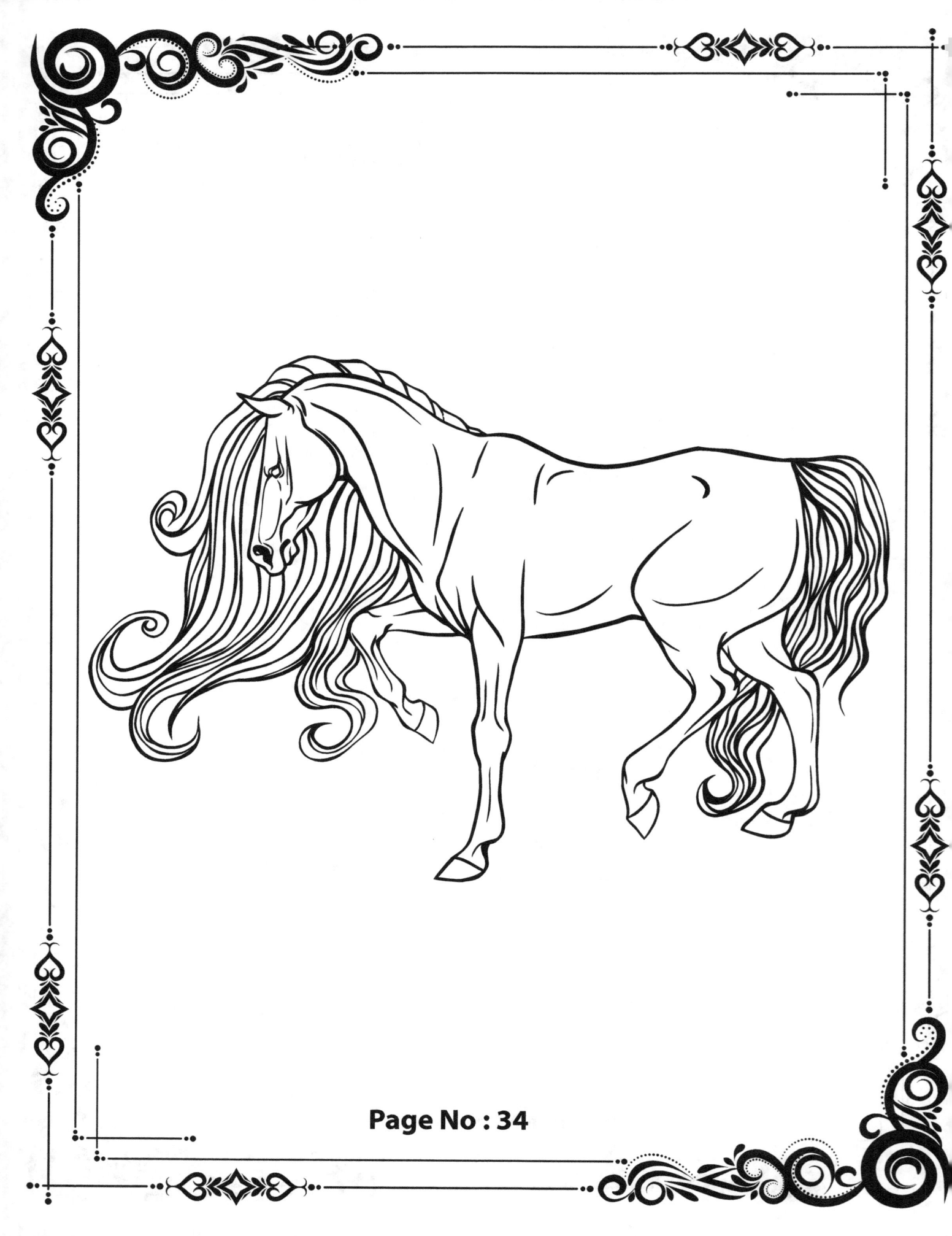

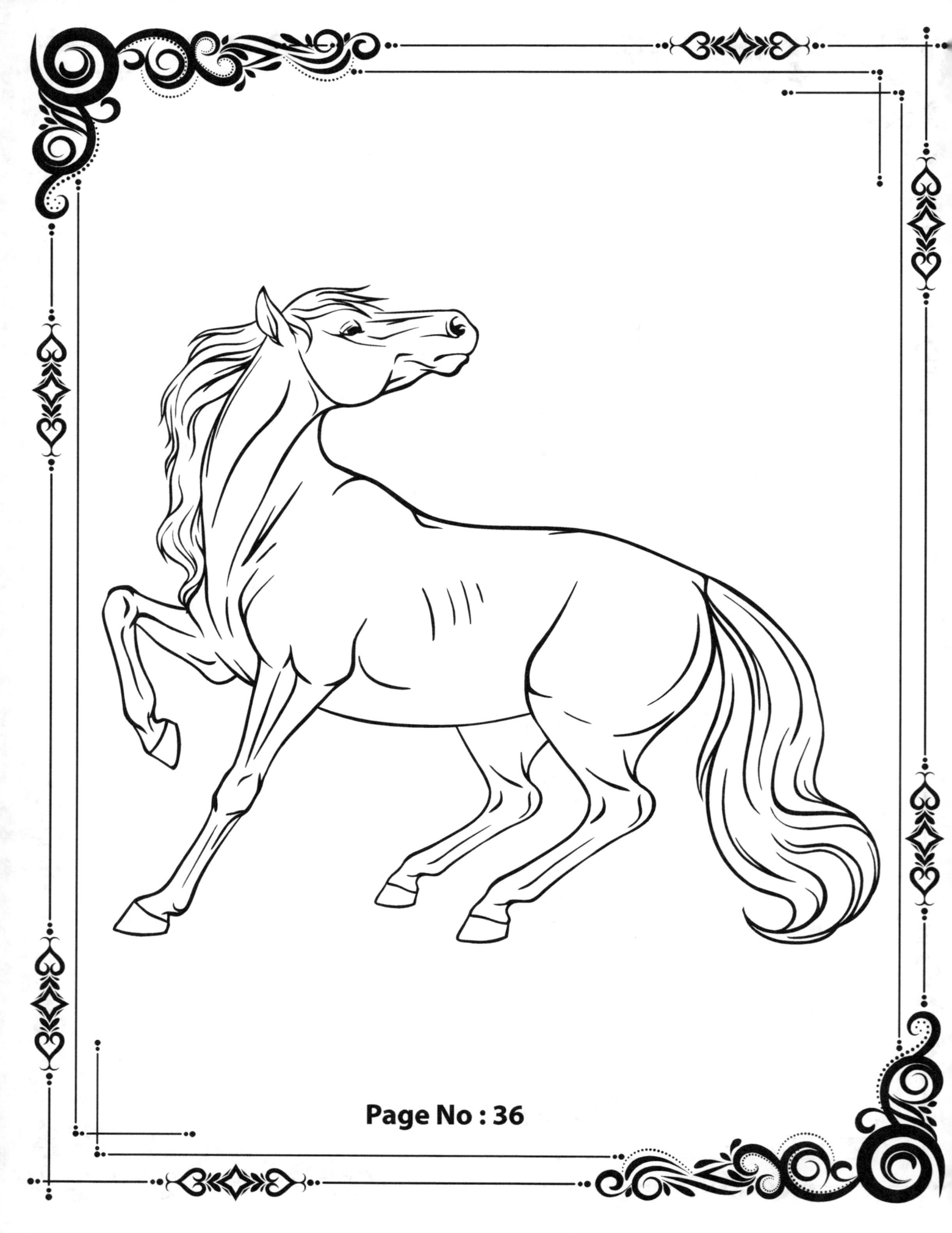

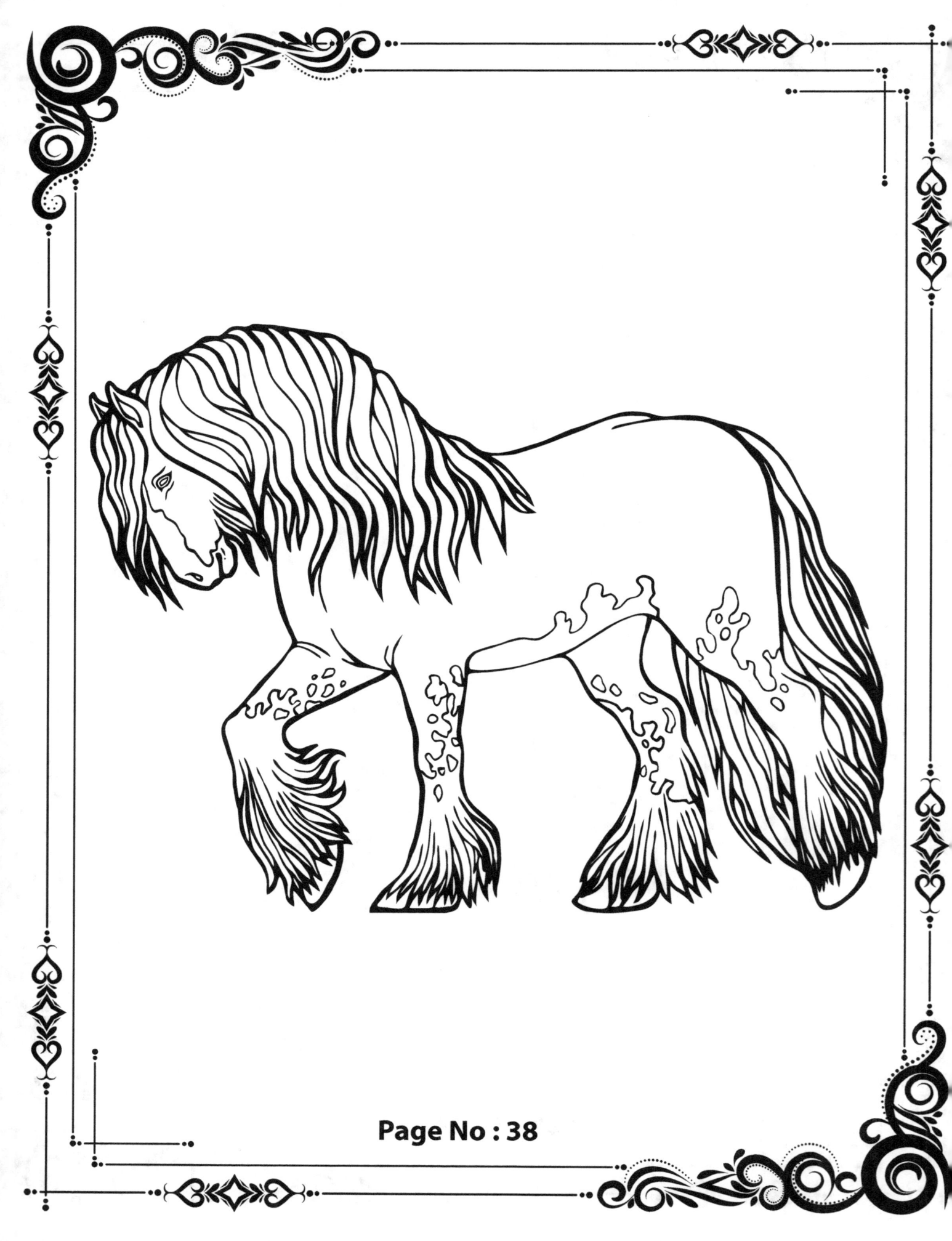

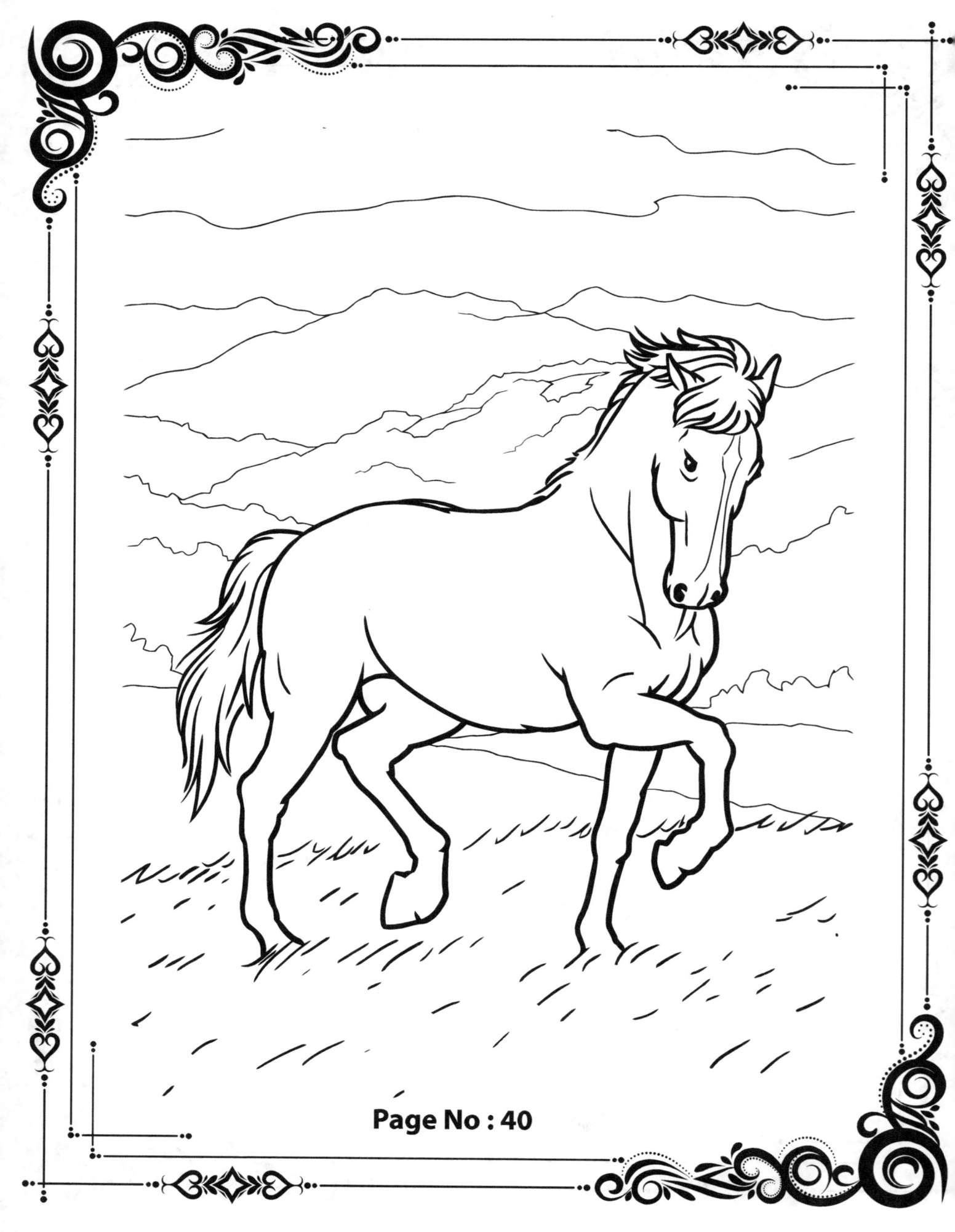

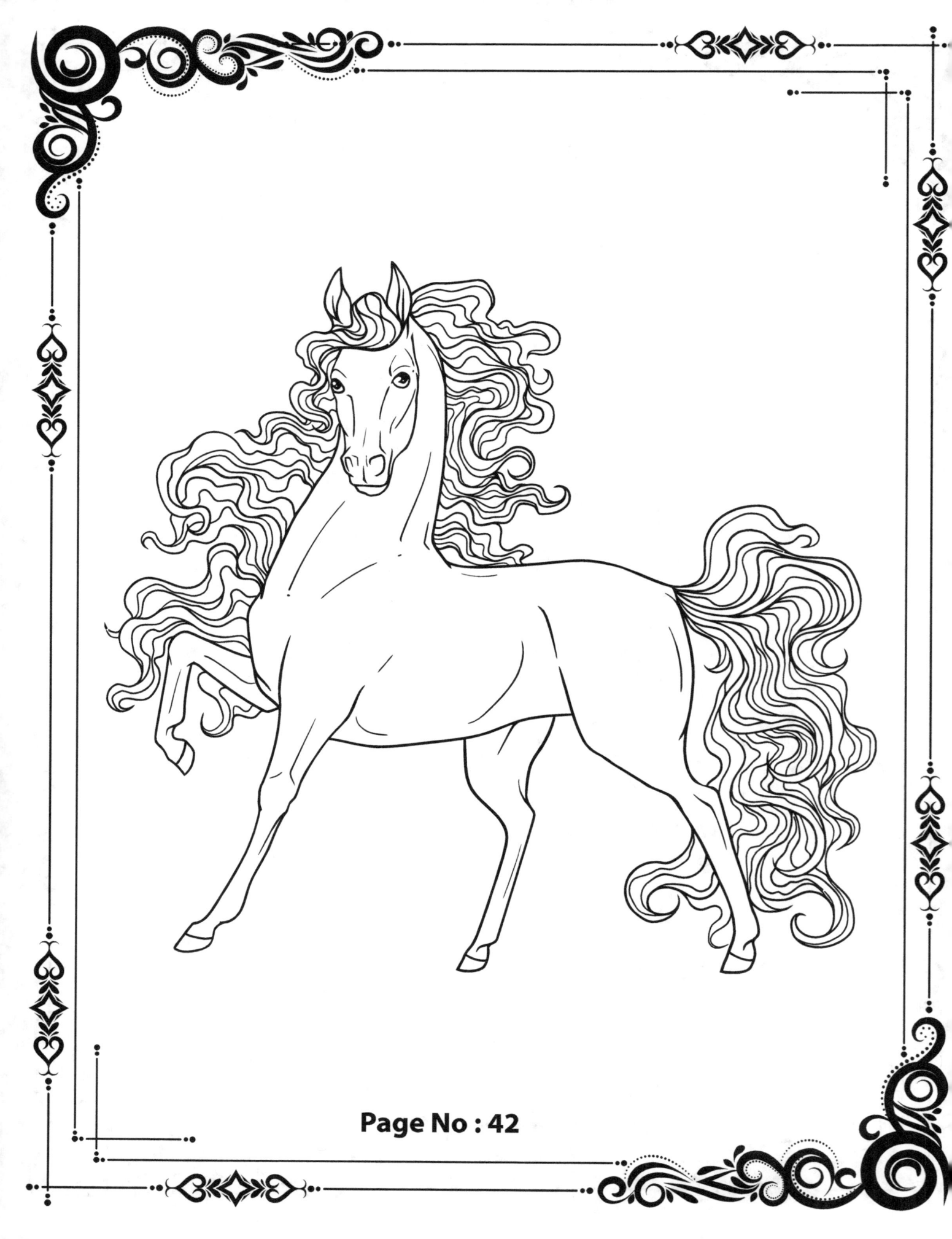

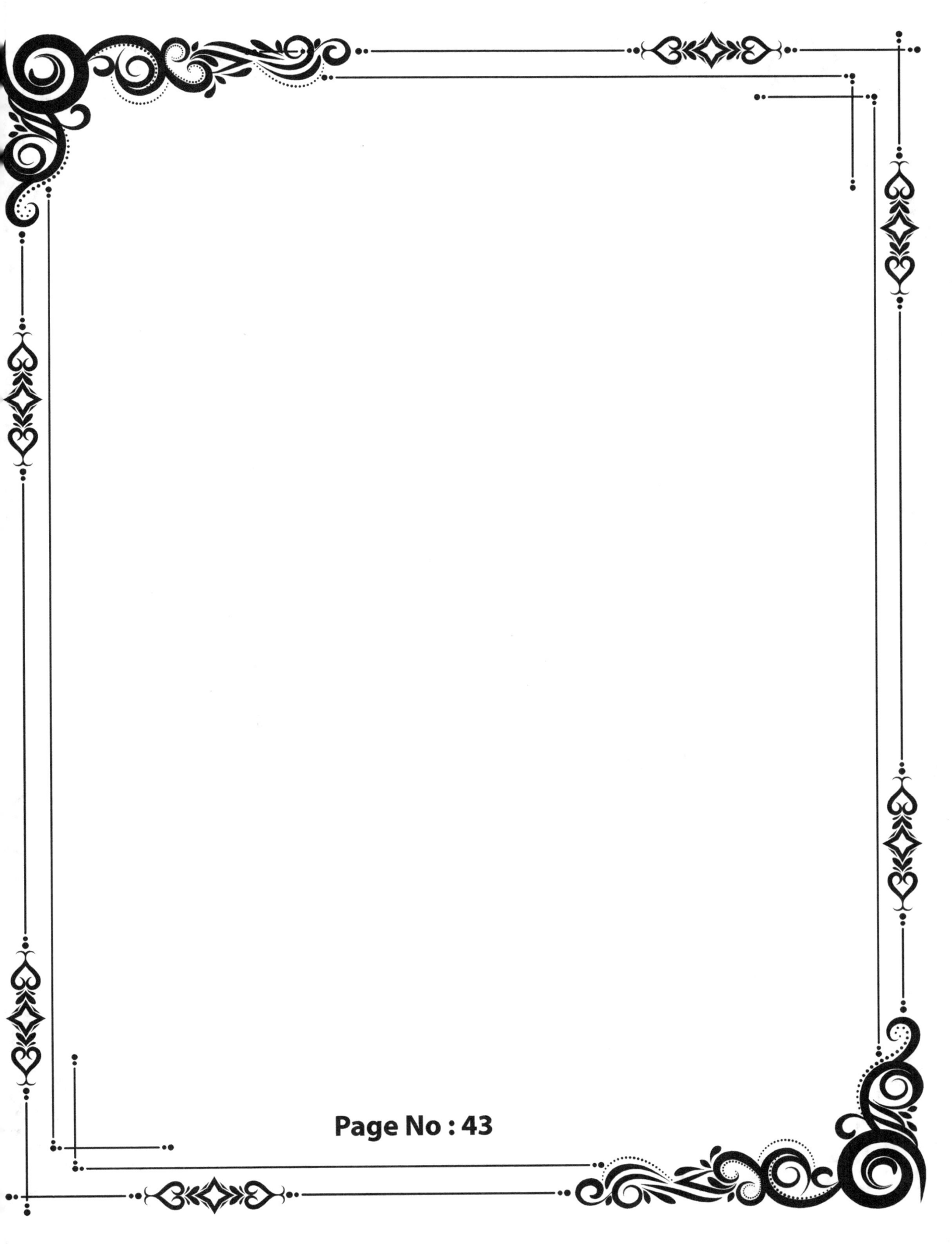

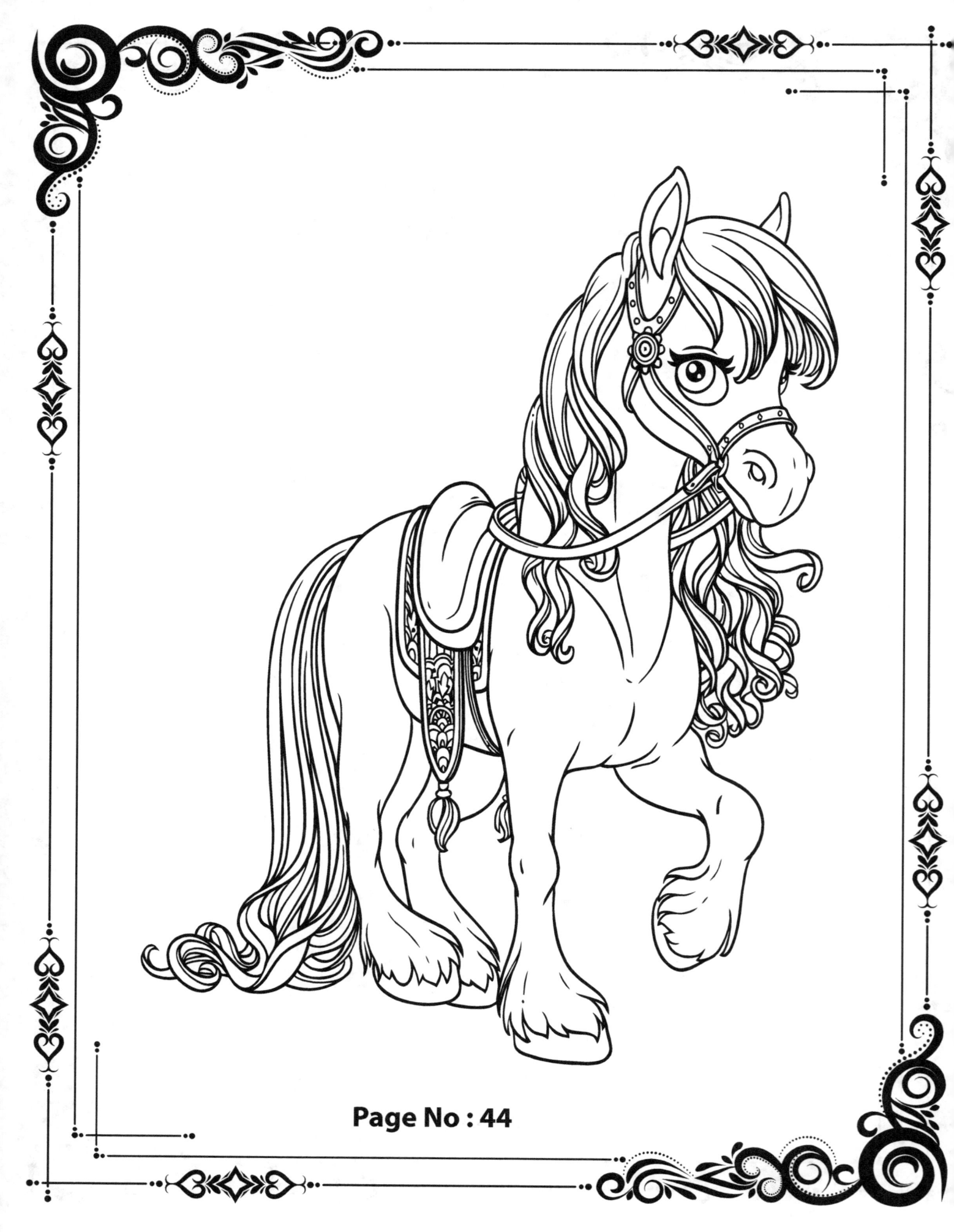

**Page No : 44**

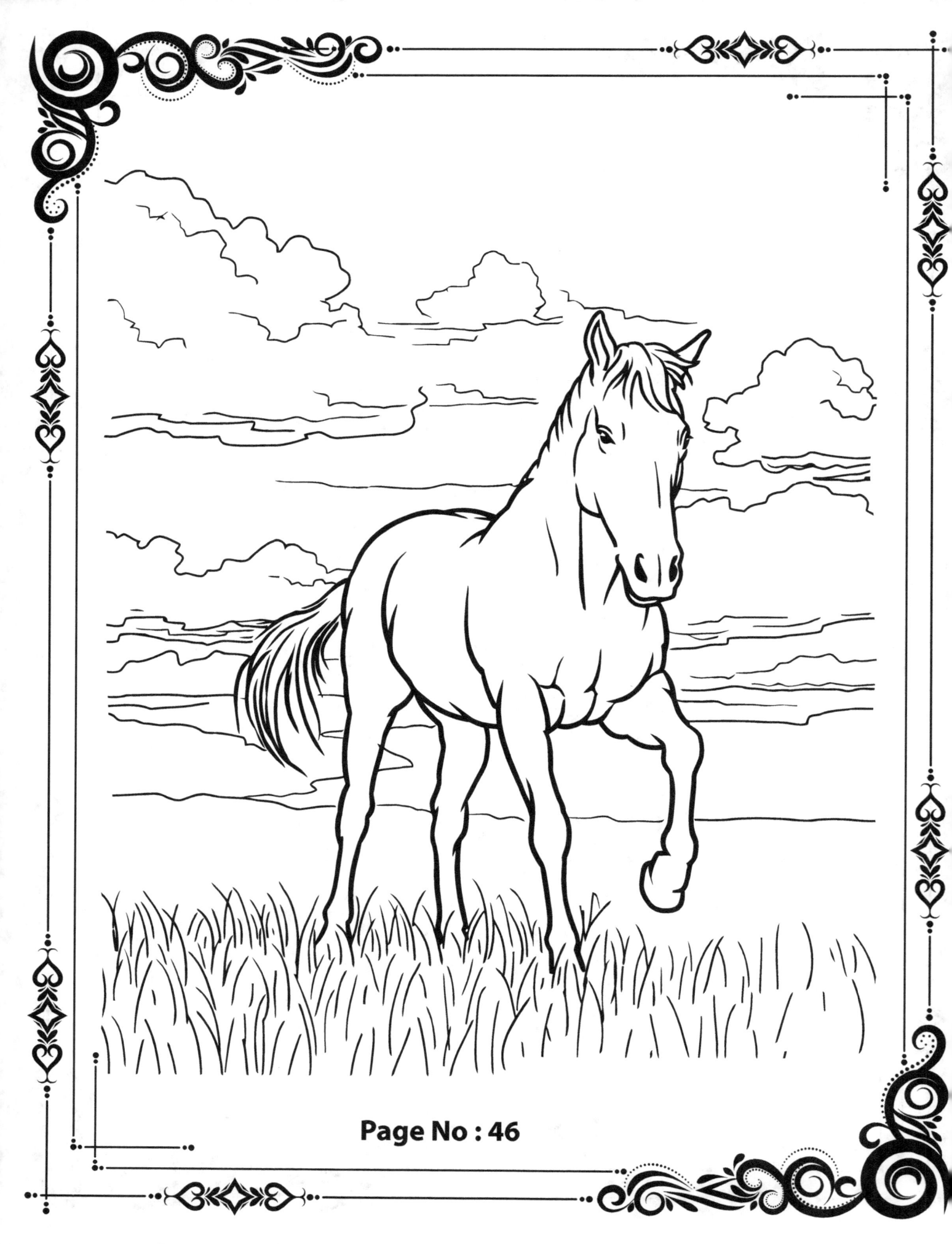

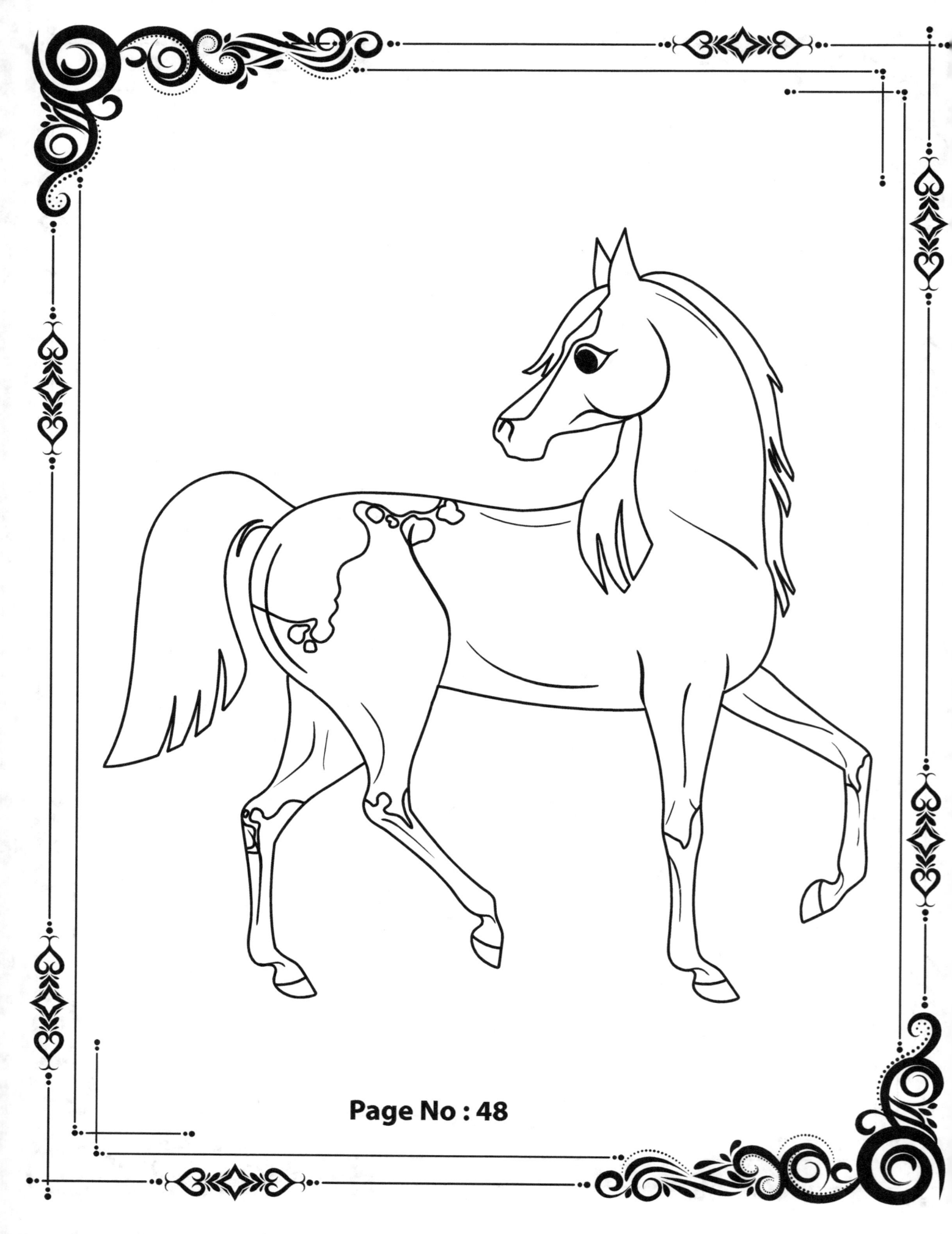

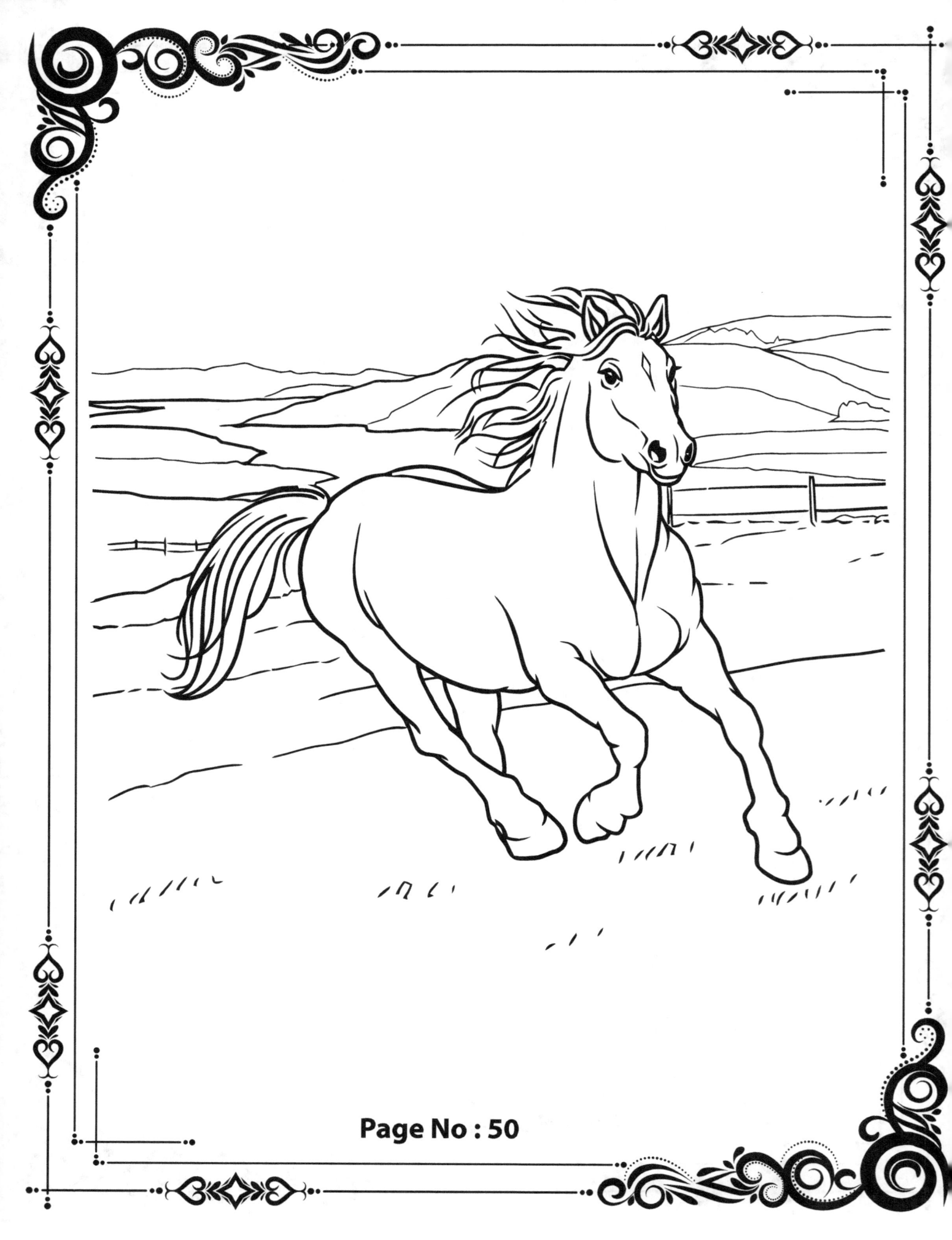

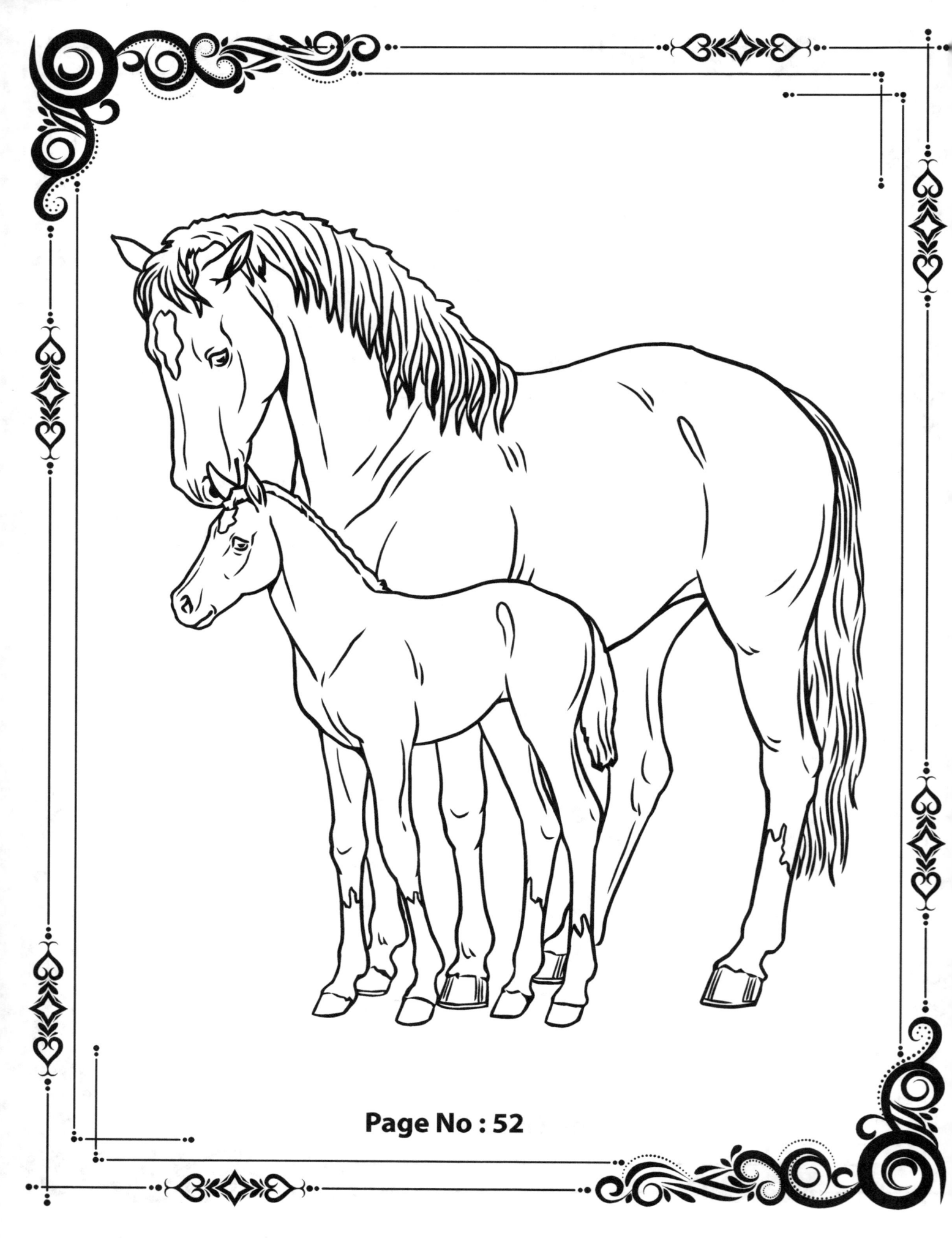

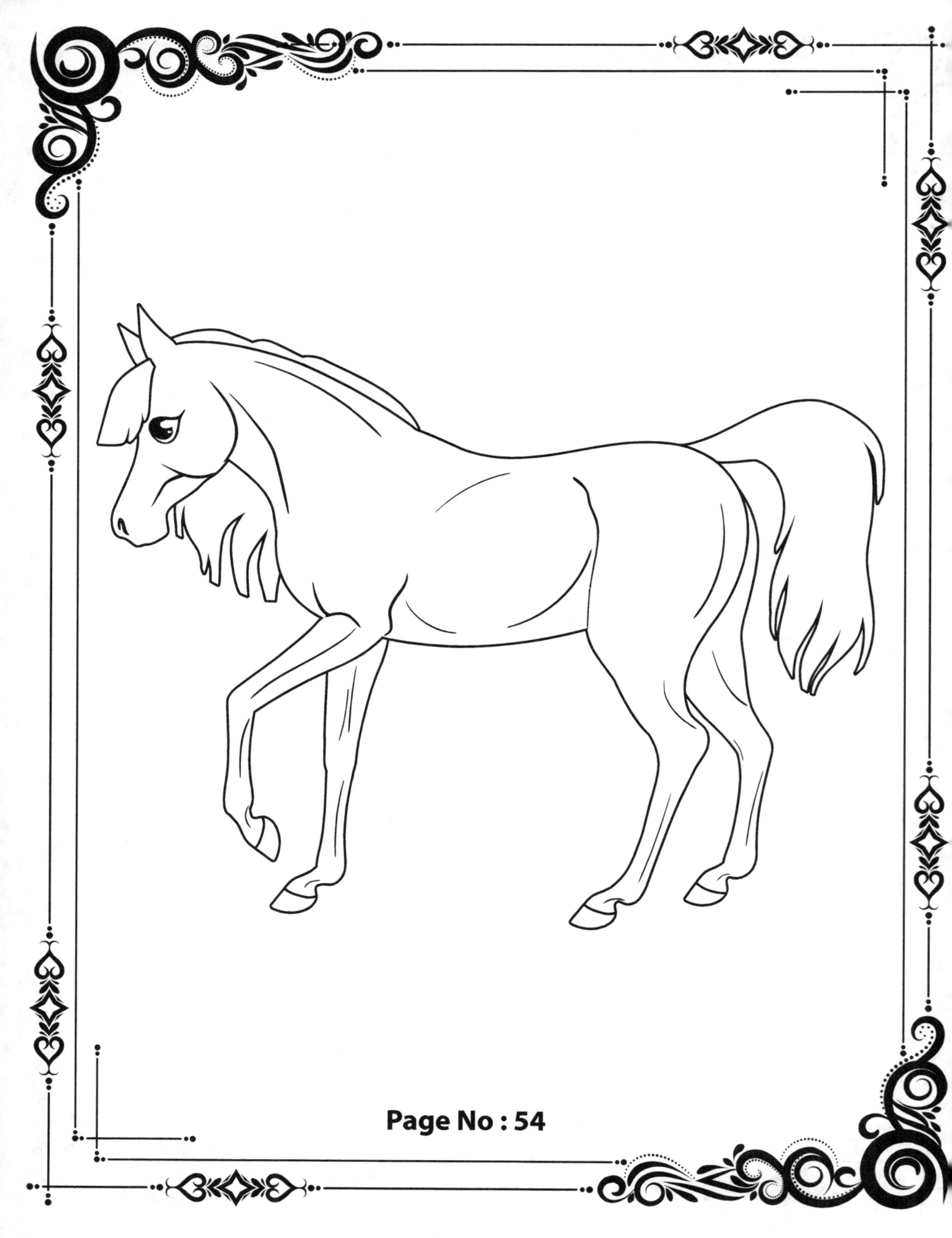

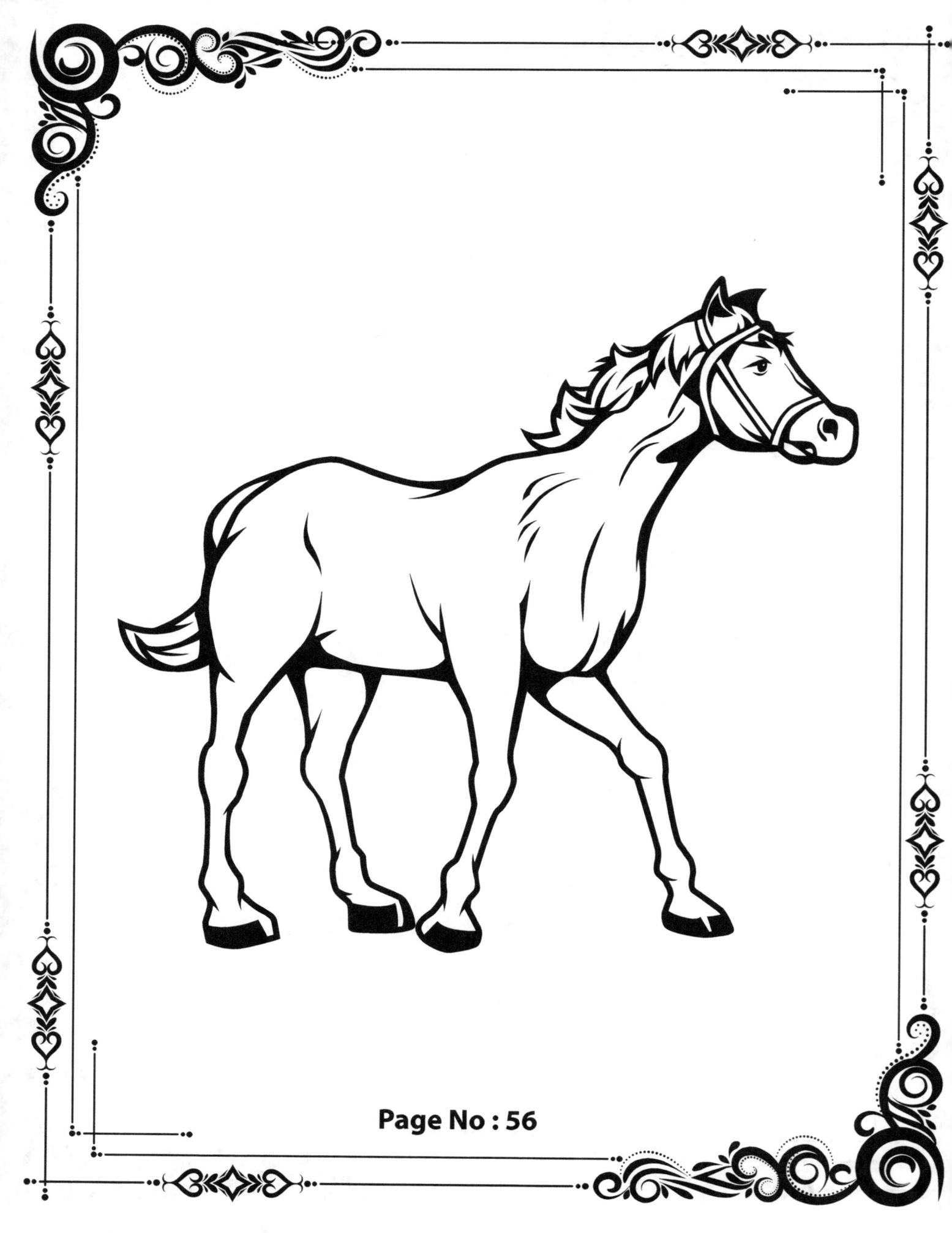

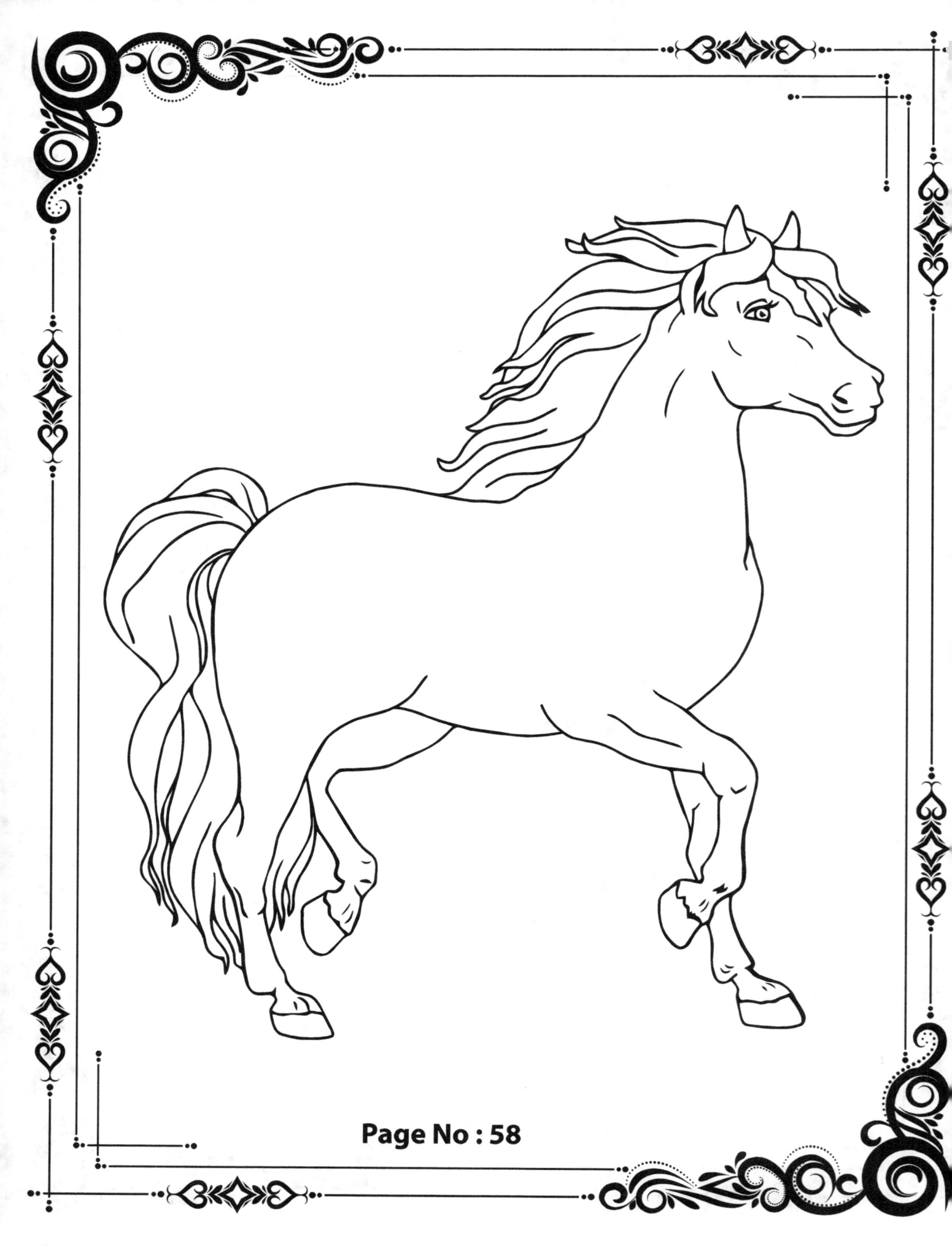

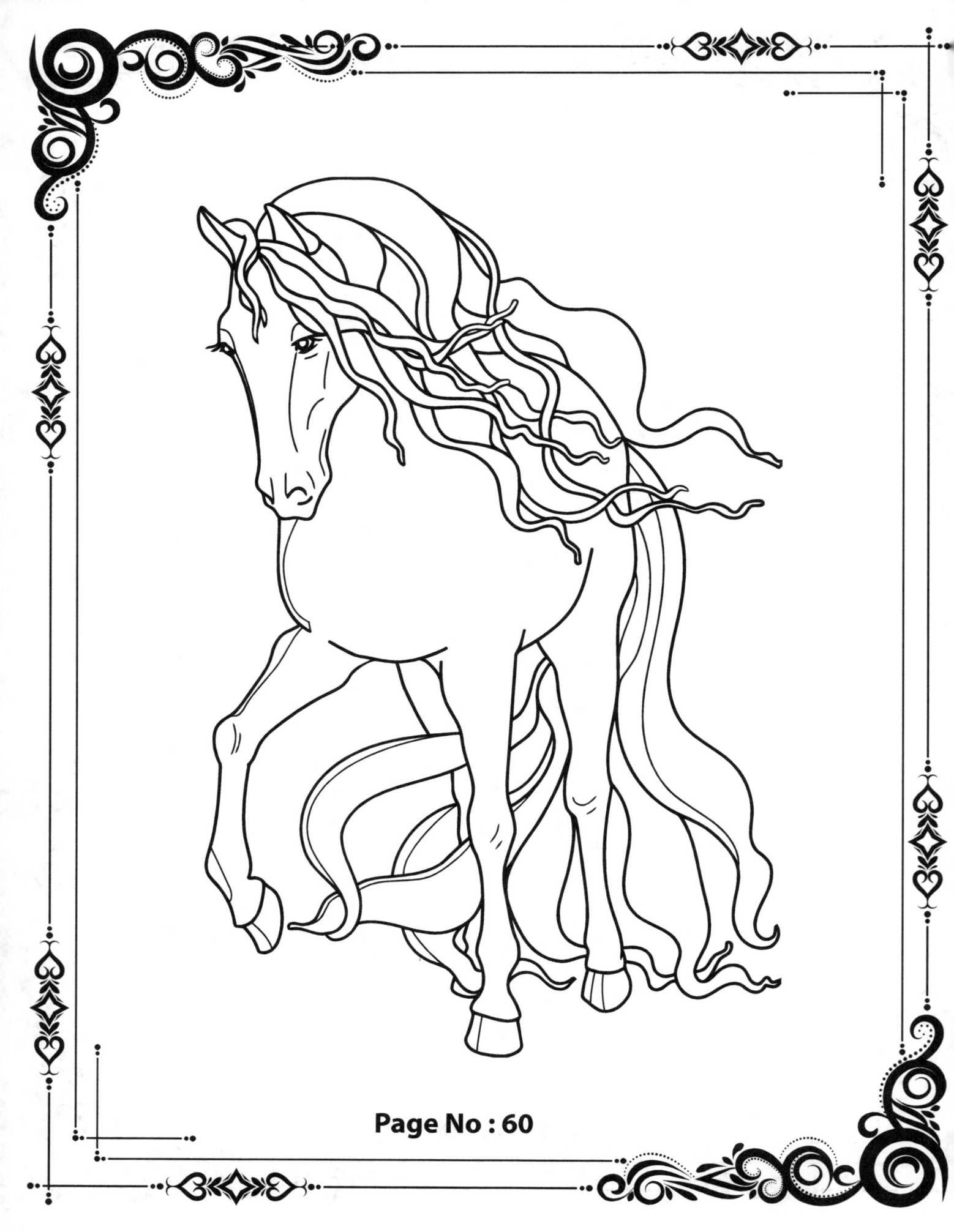

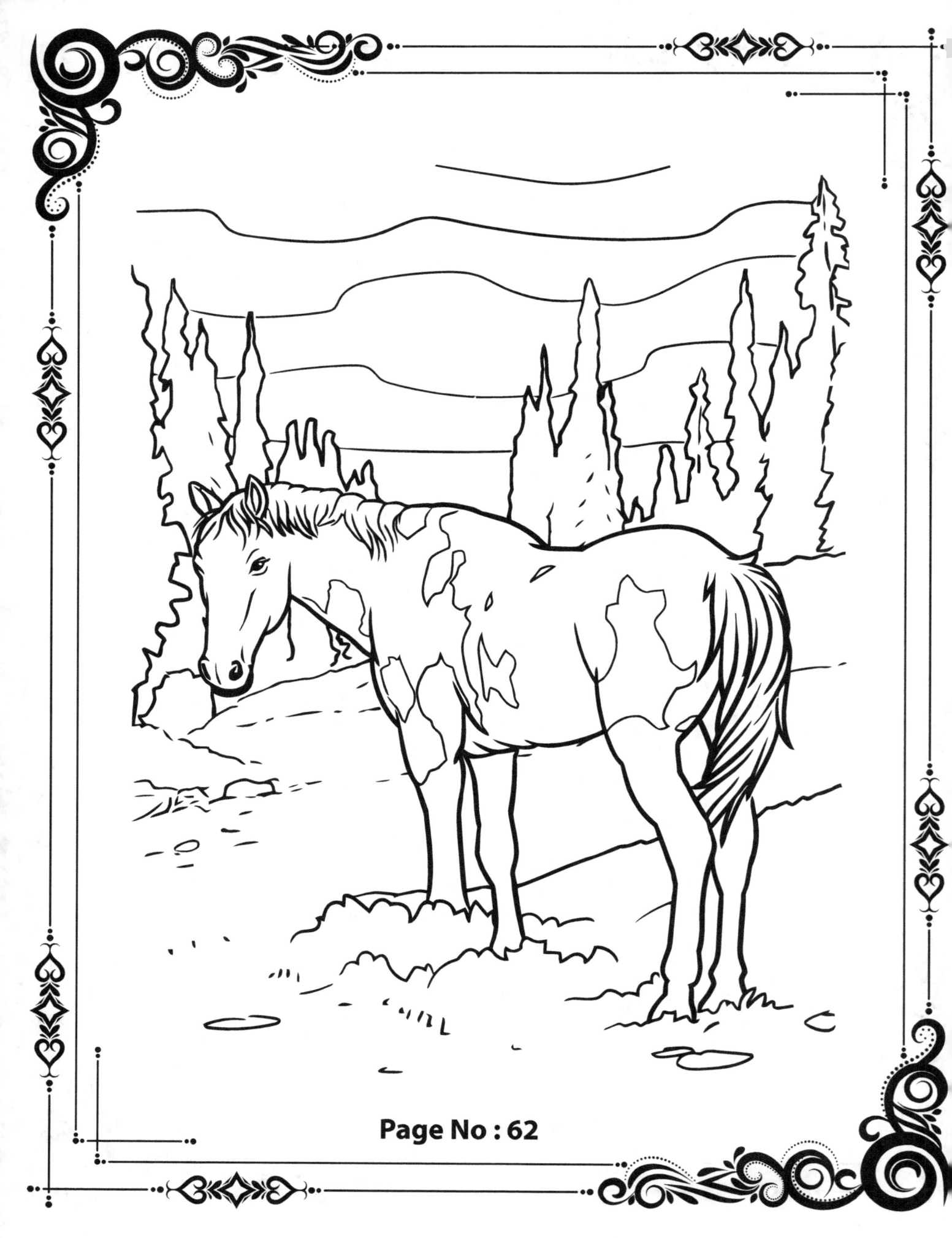

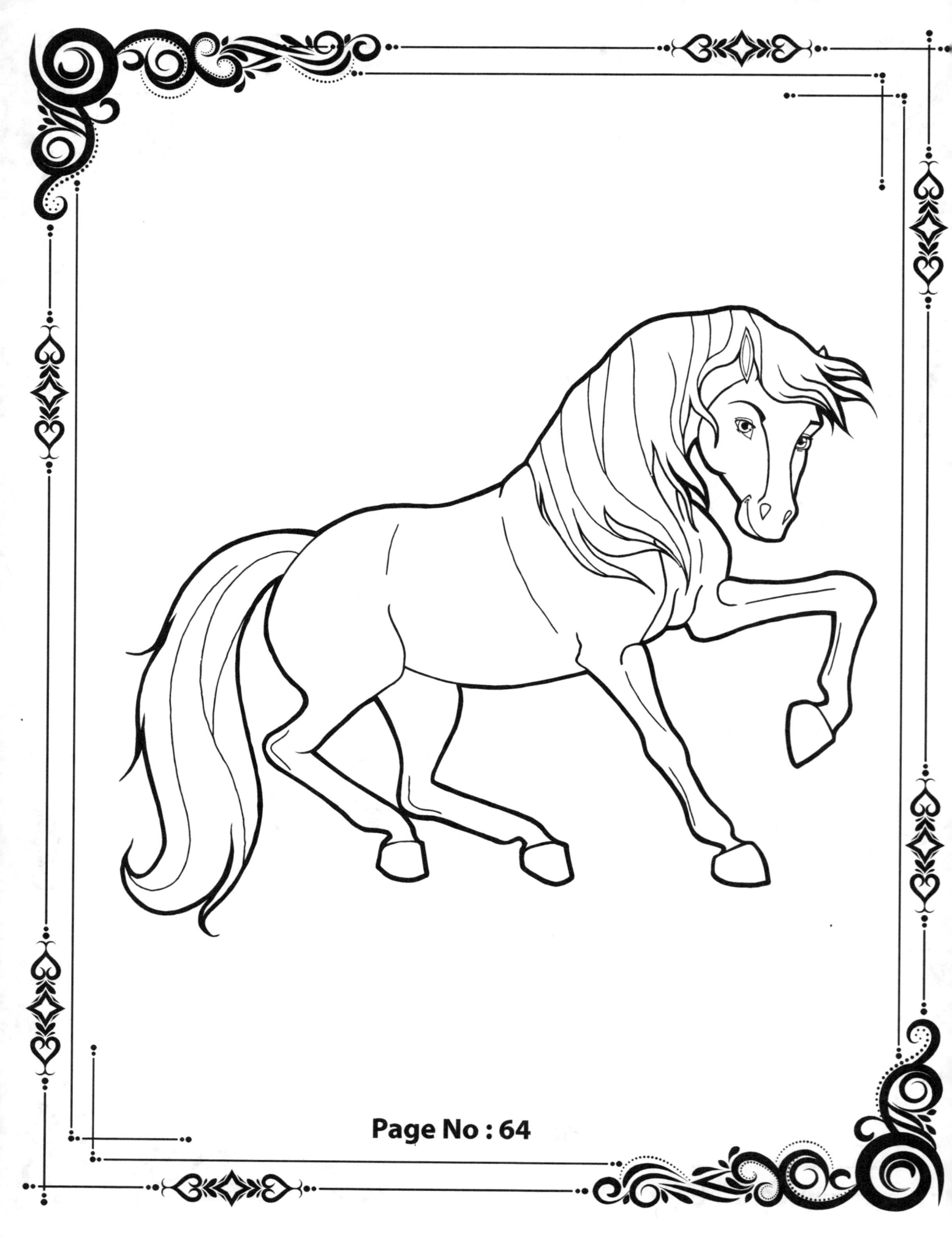

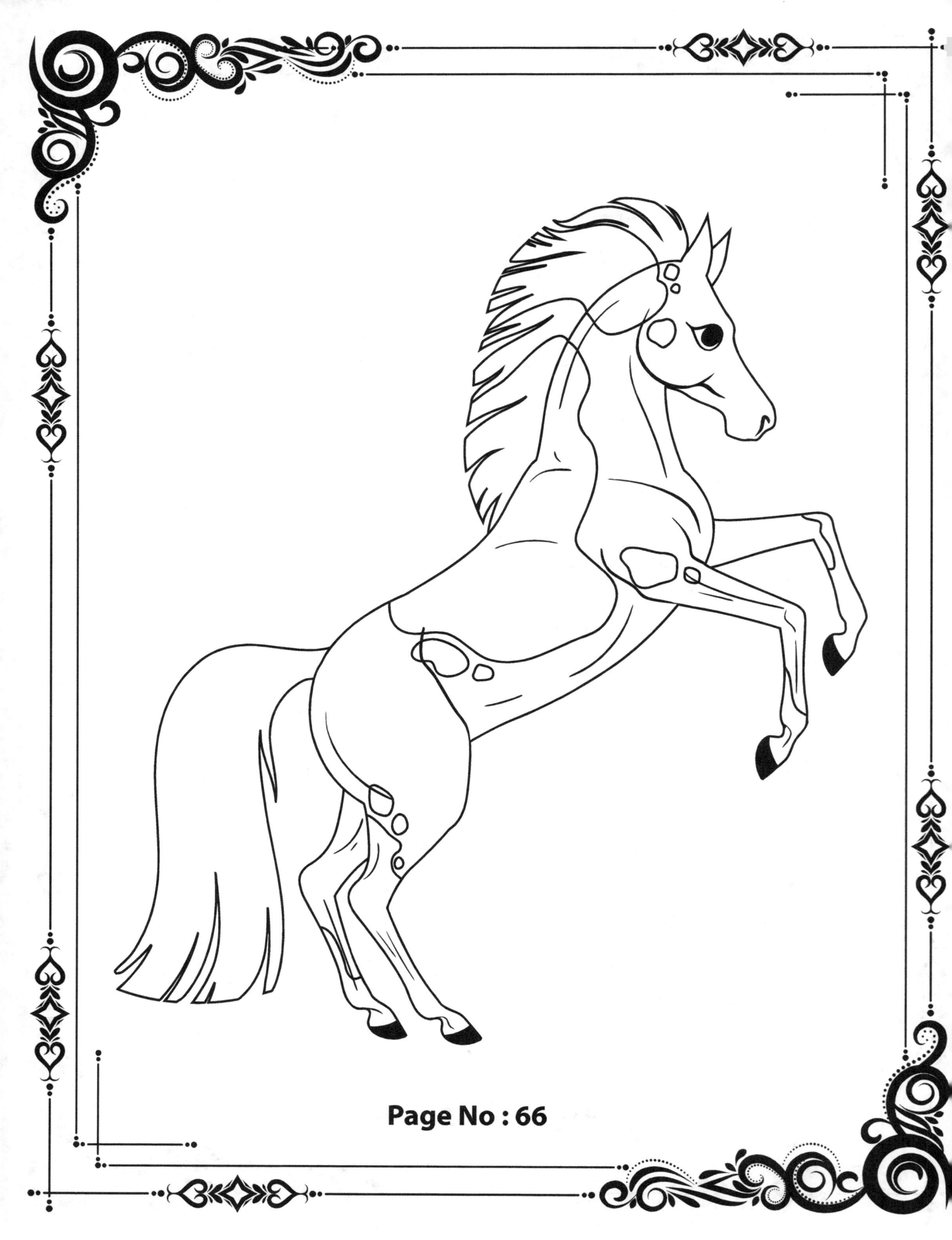

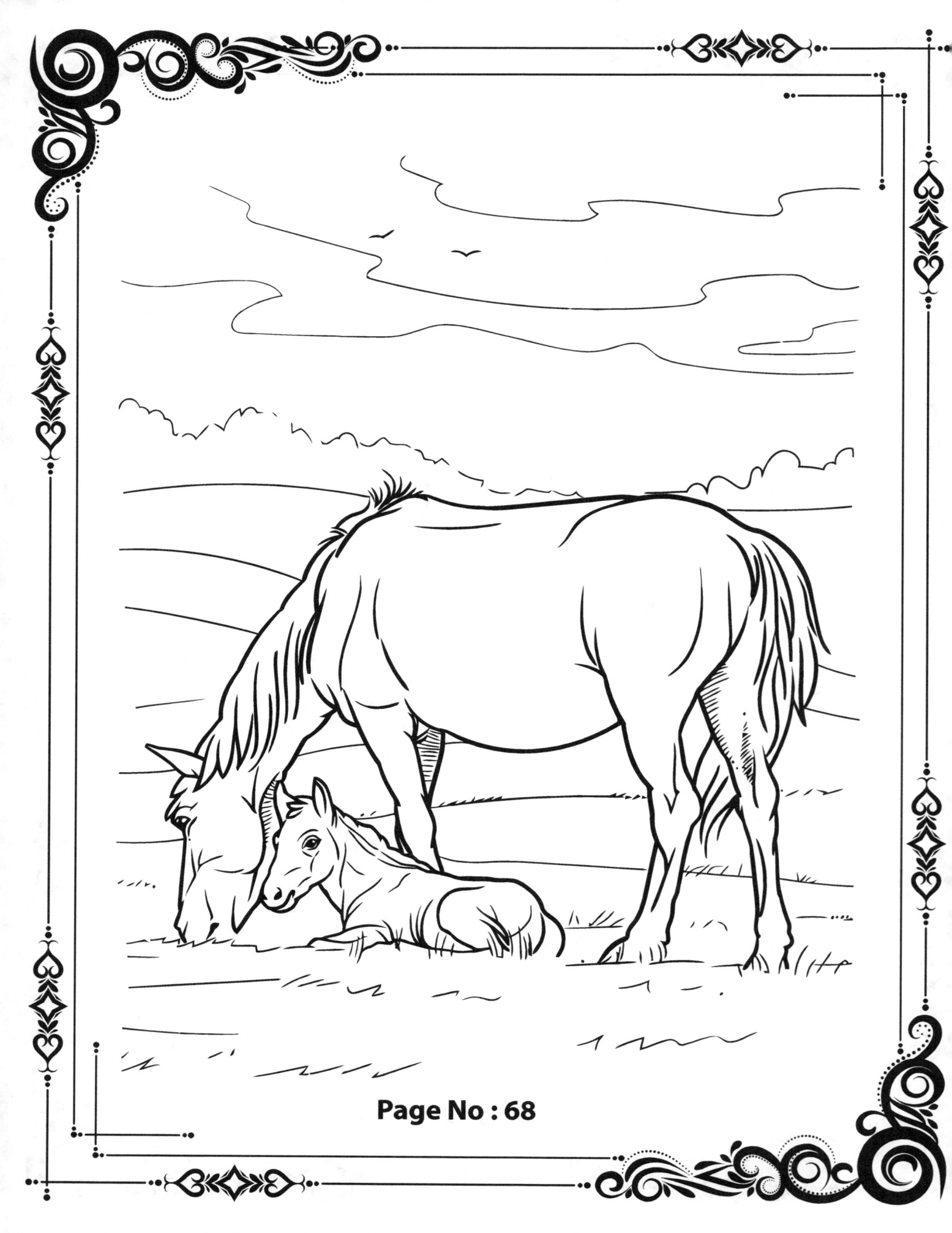

**Page No : 68**

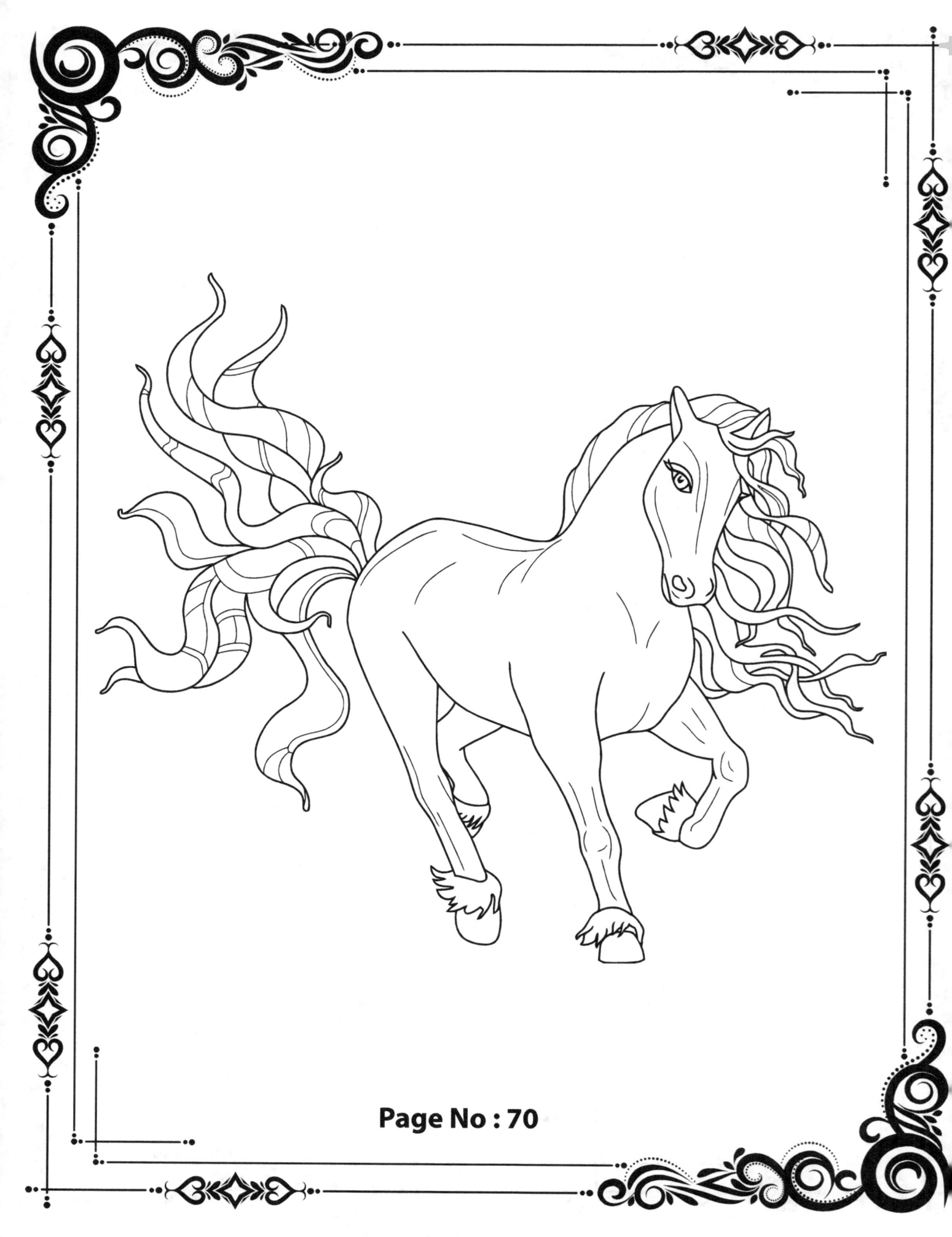

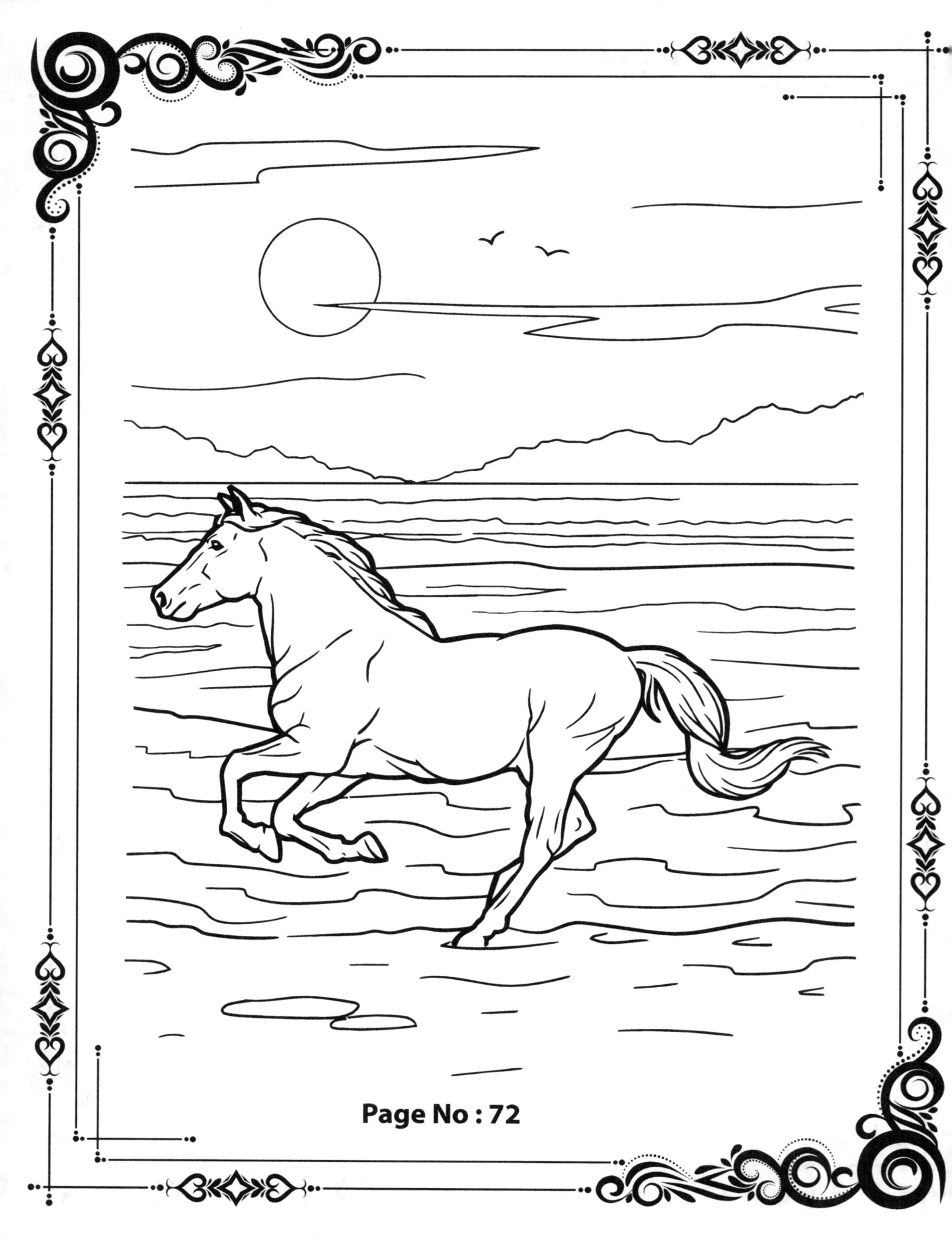

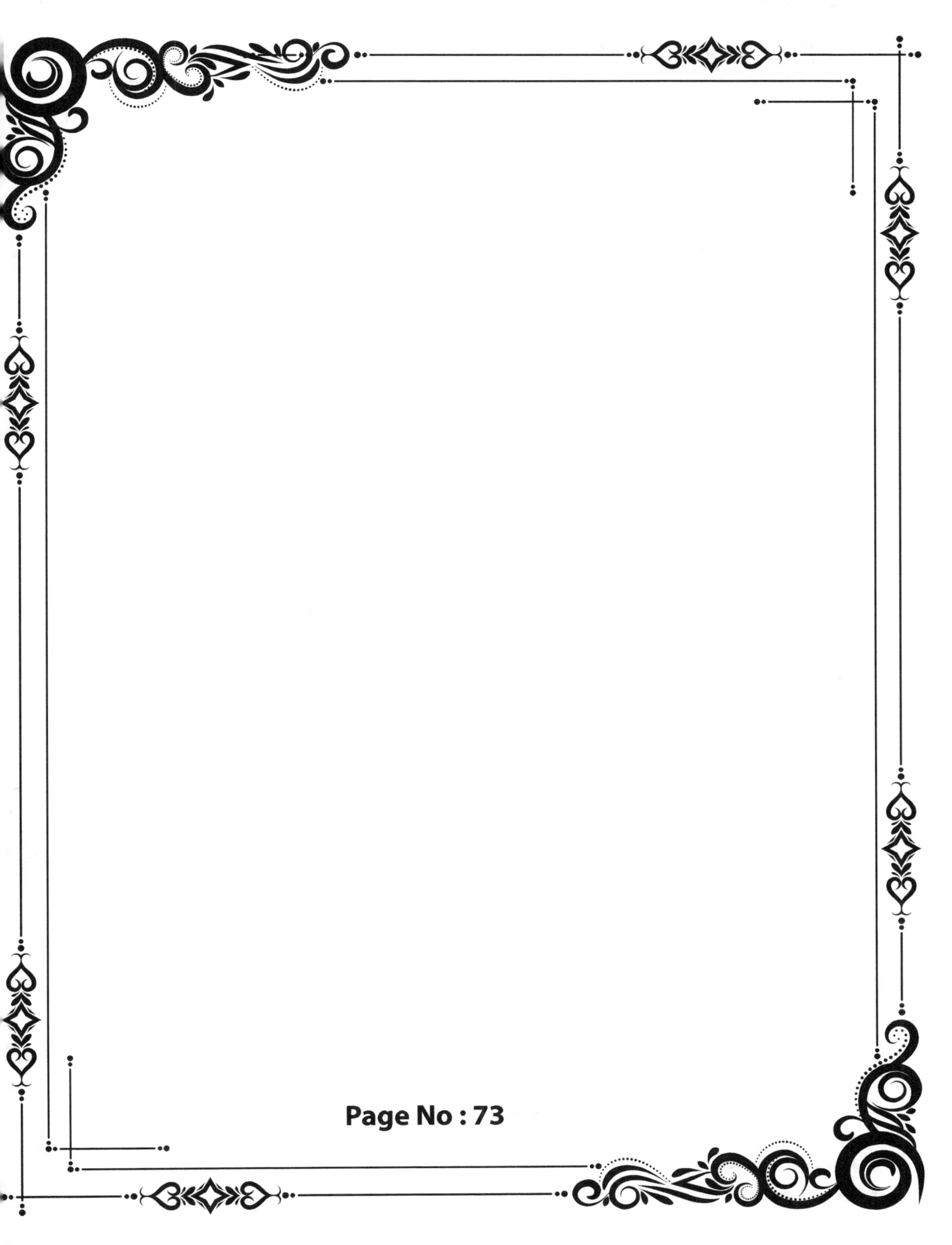

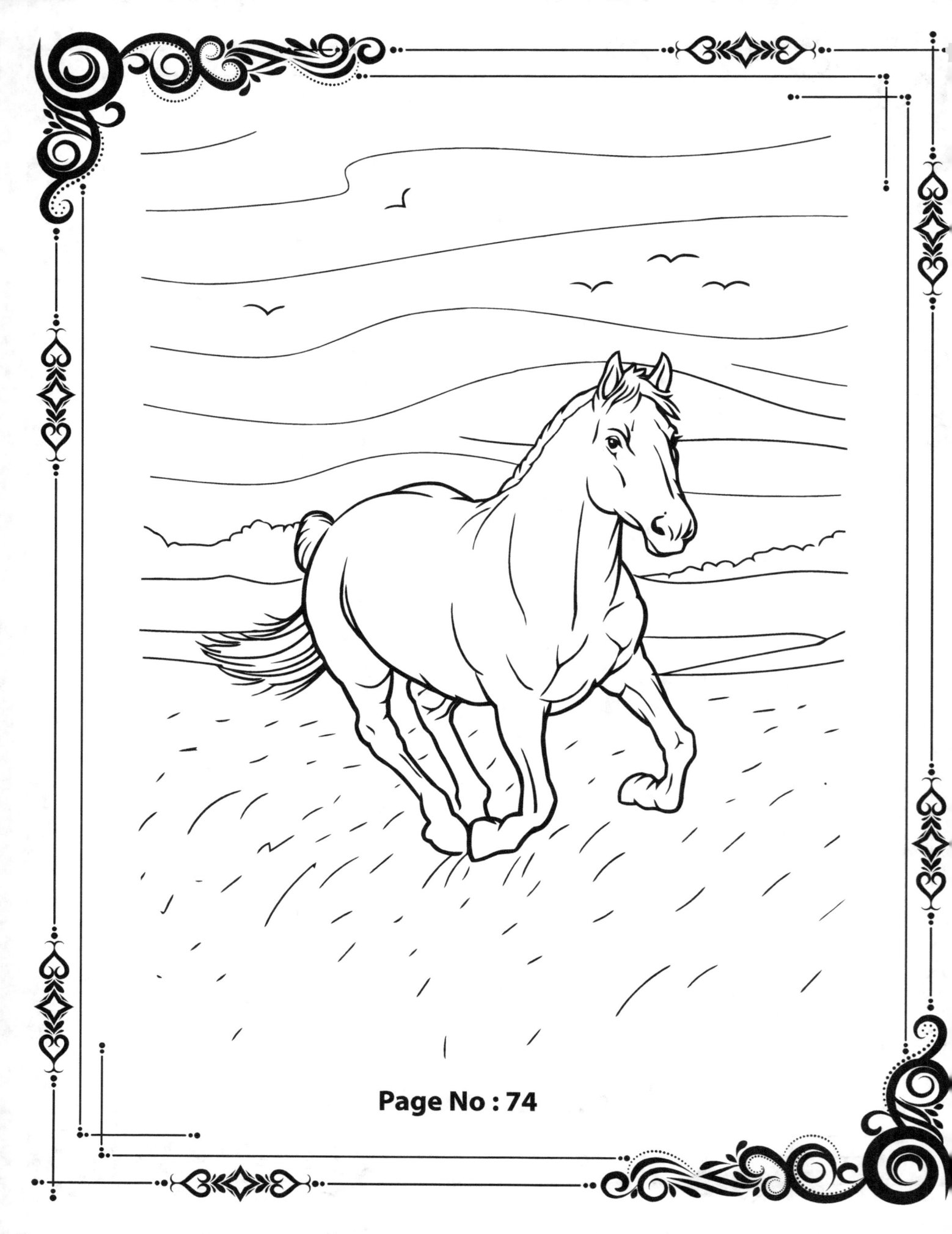

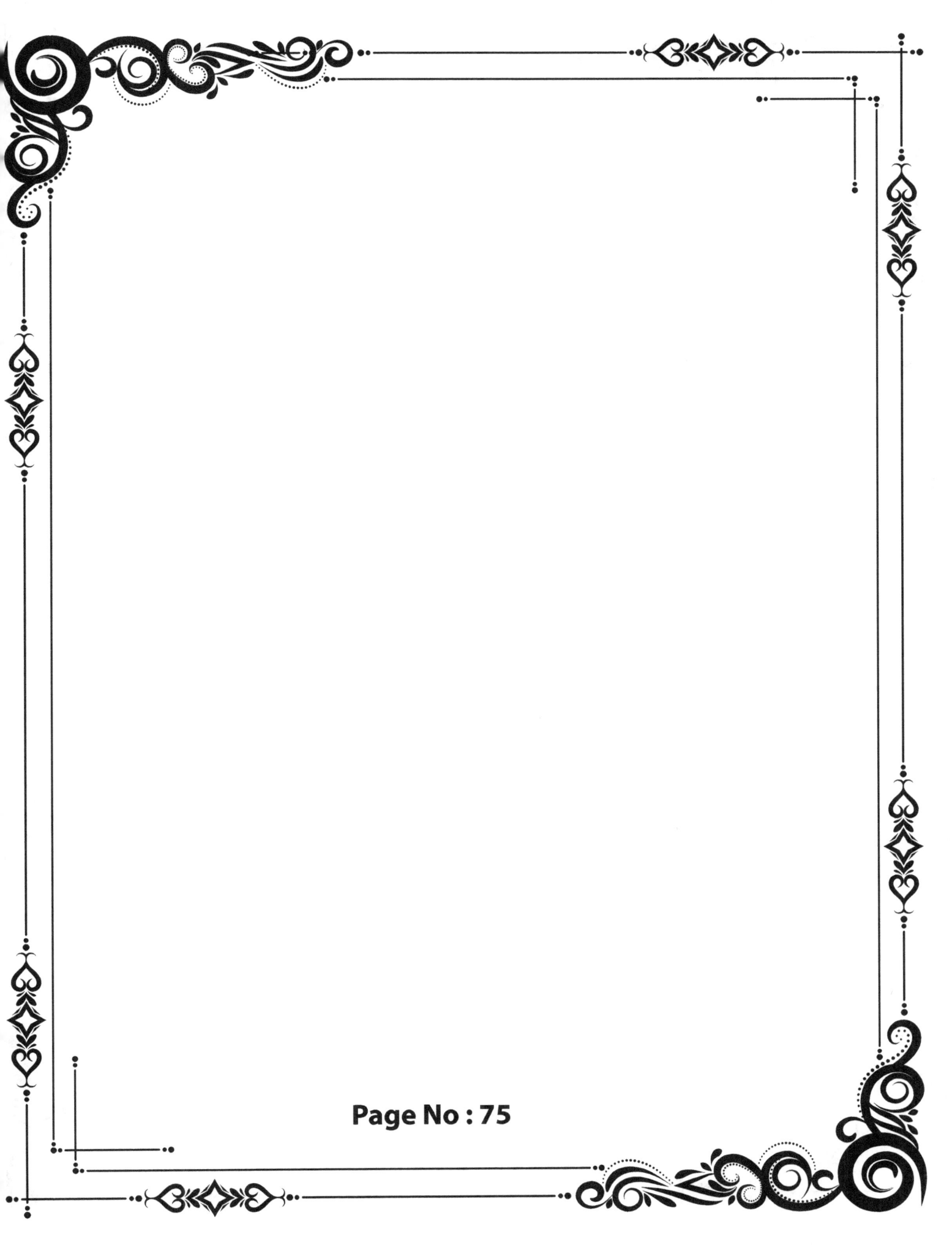

Page No : 75

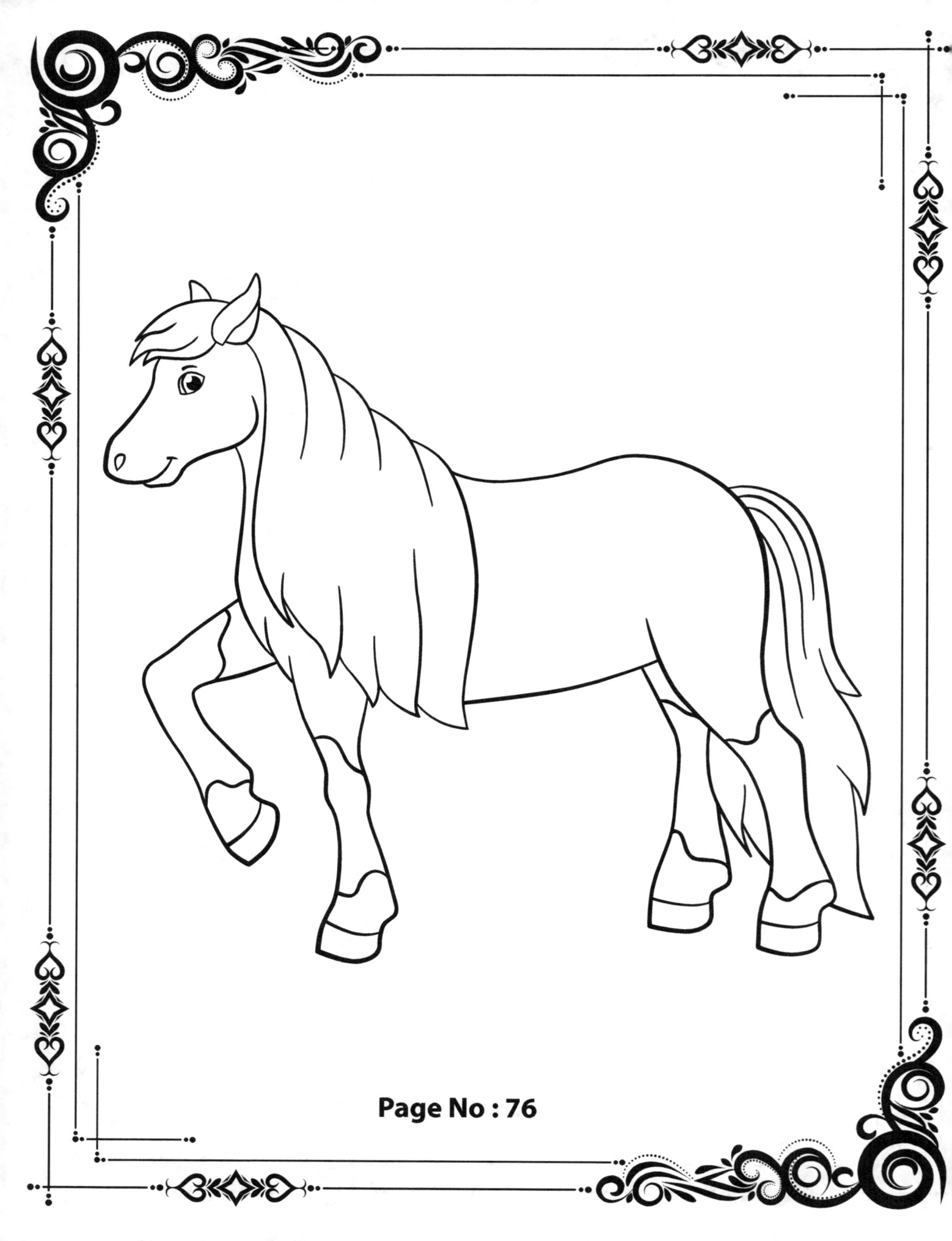

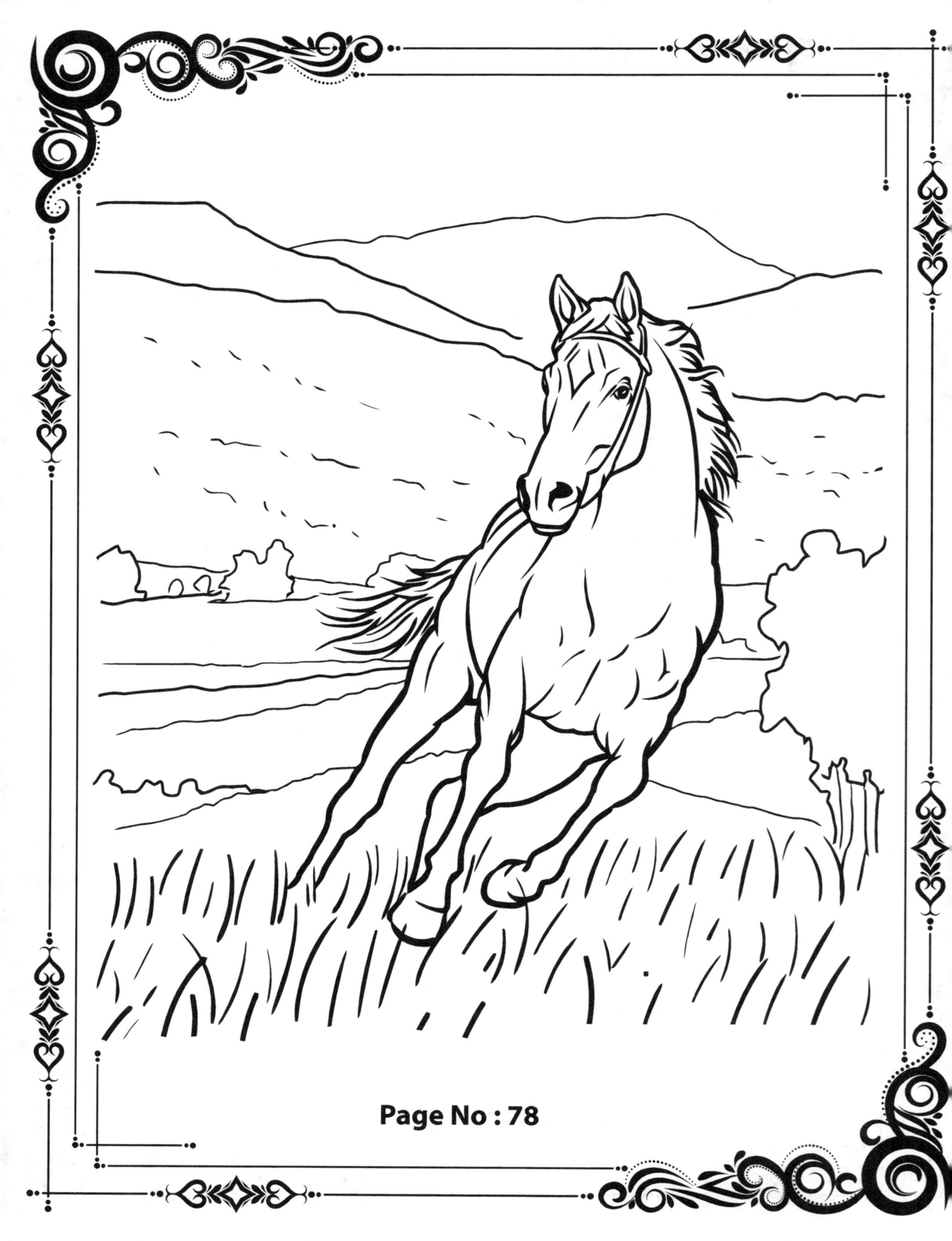

**Page No : 78**

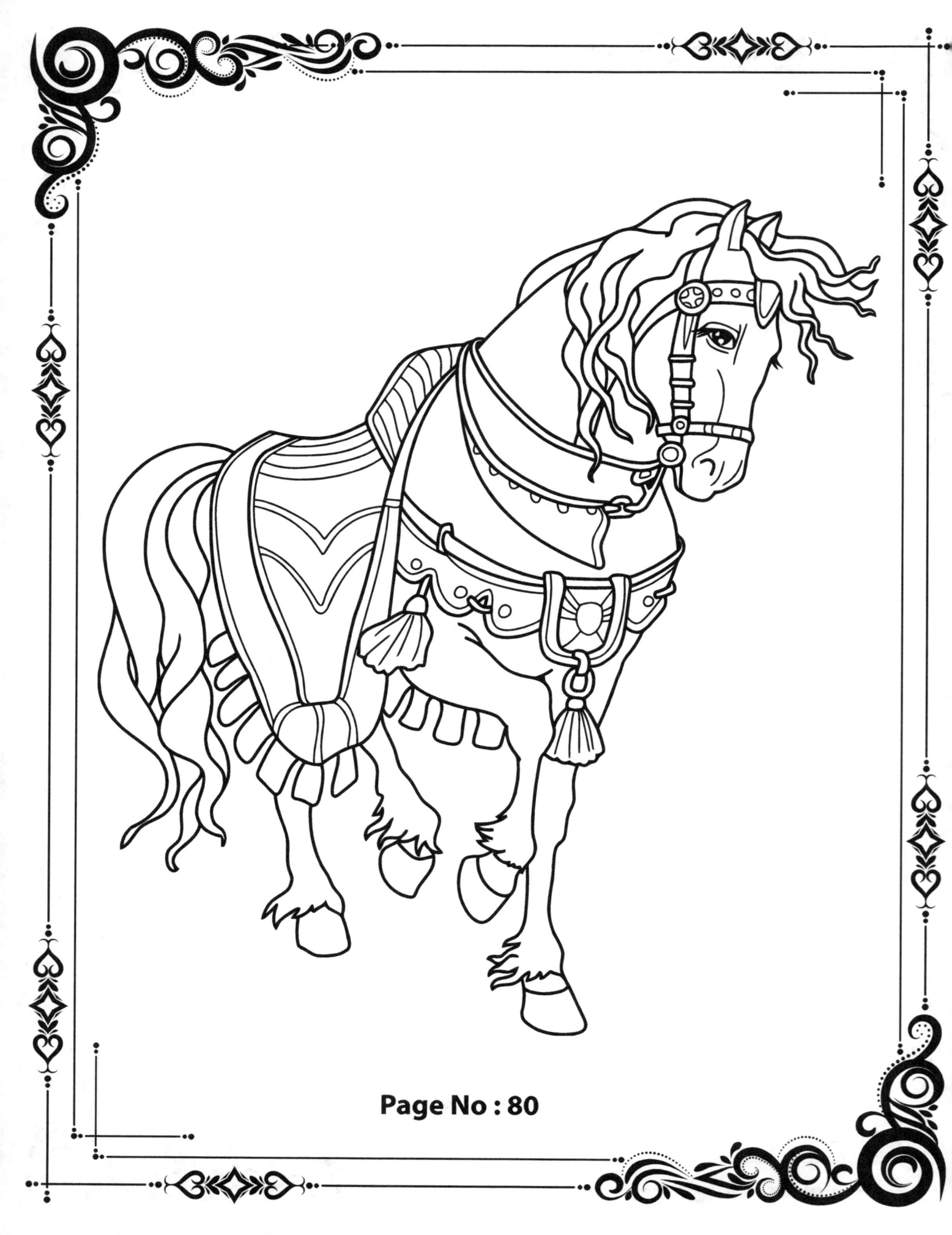

**Page No : 80**

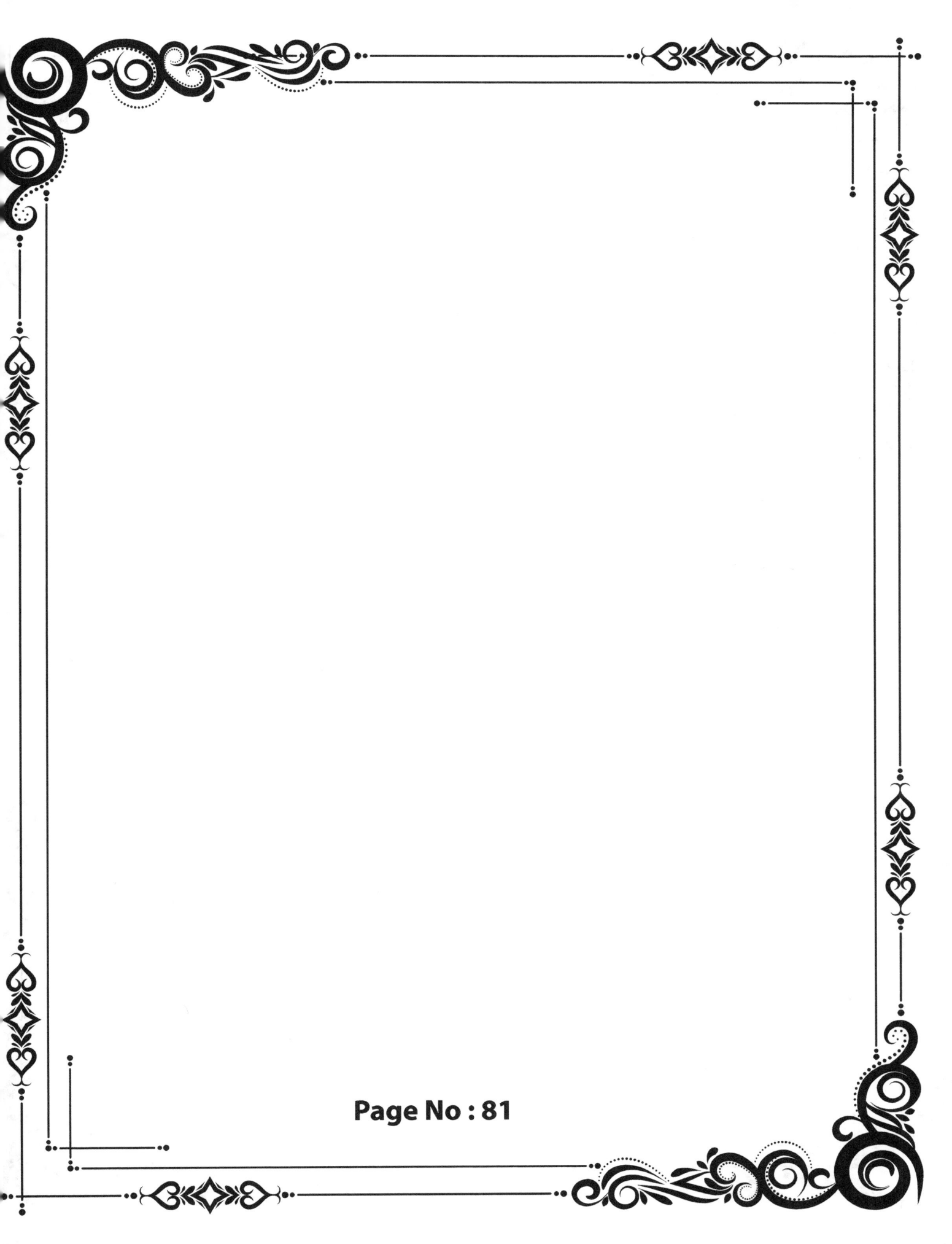

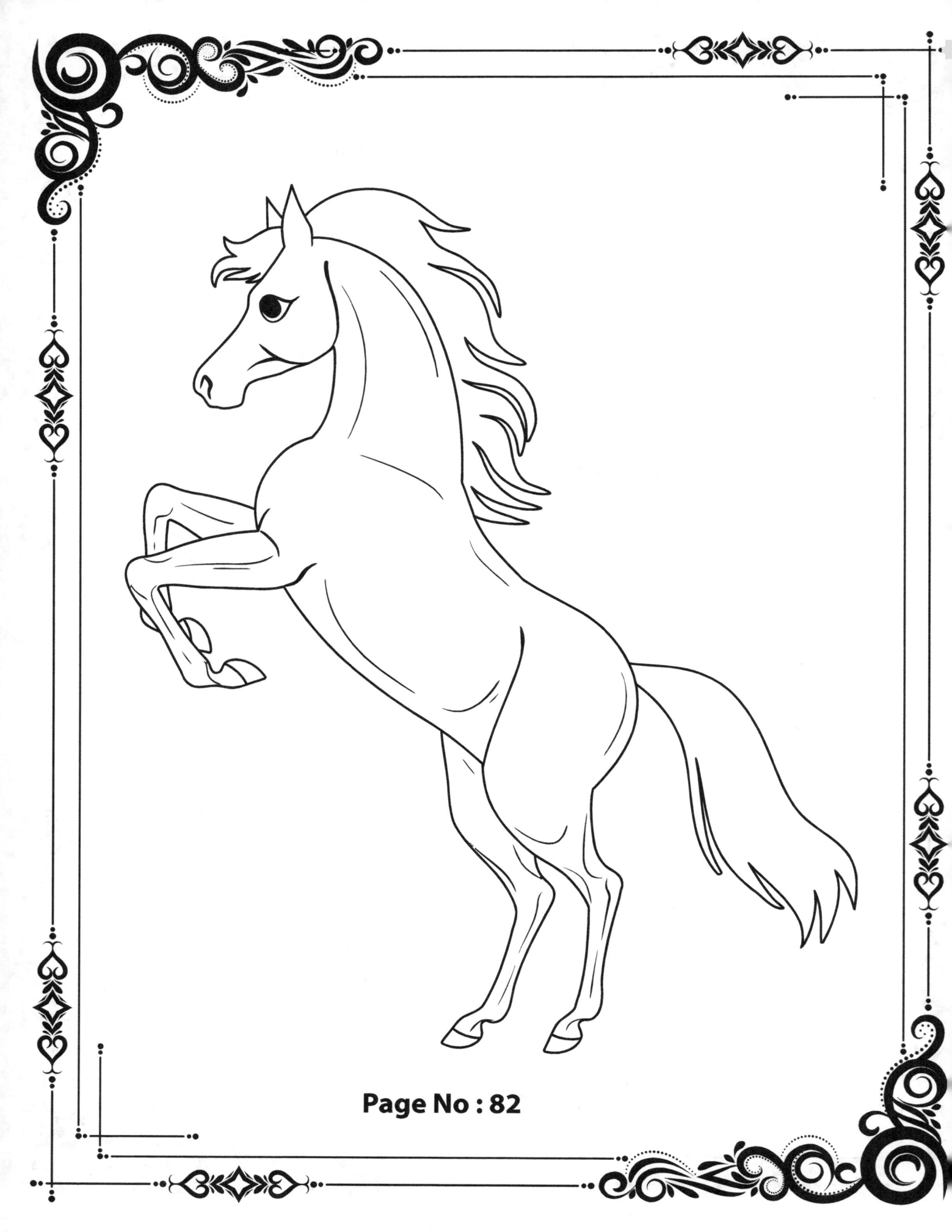

**Page No : 82**

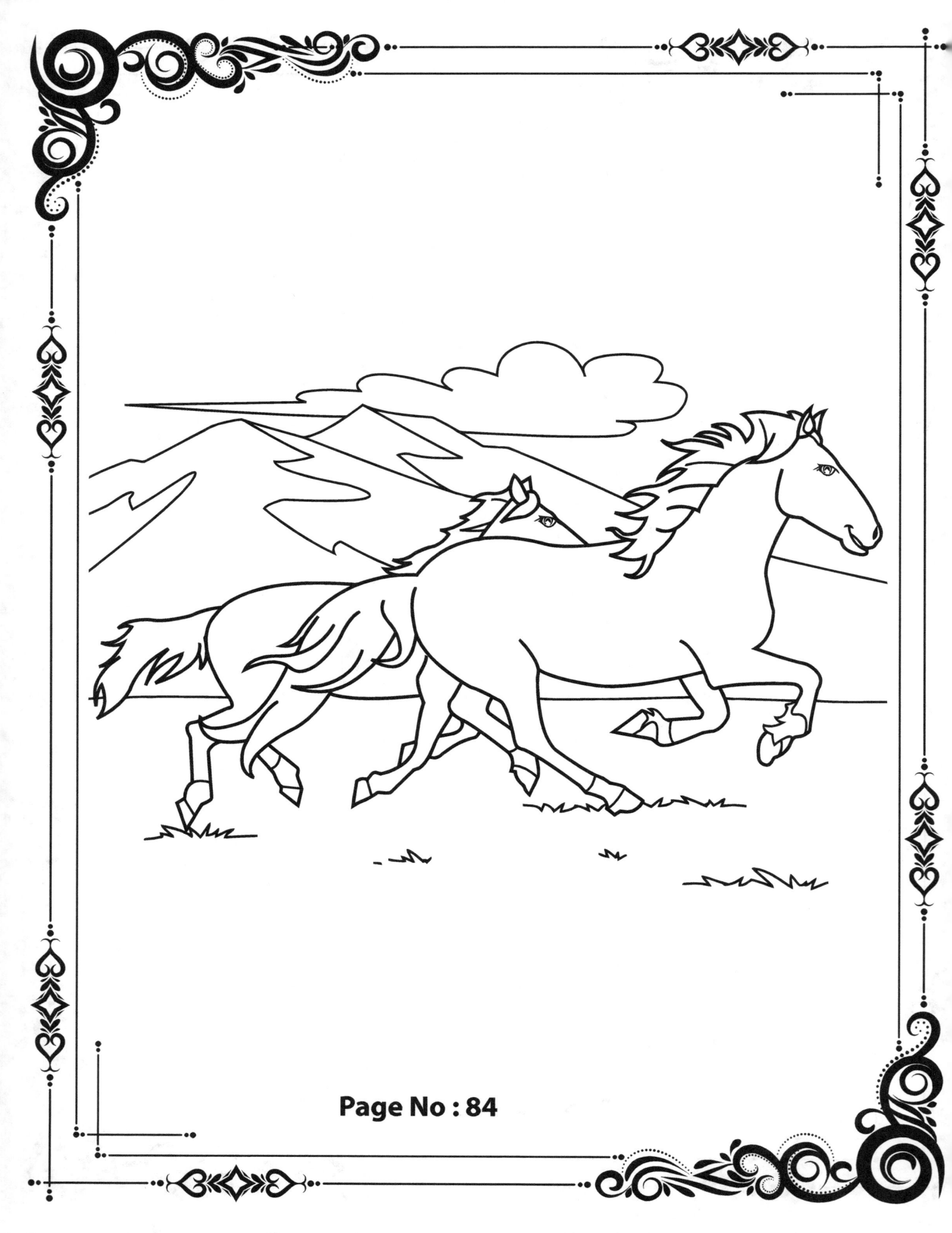

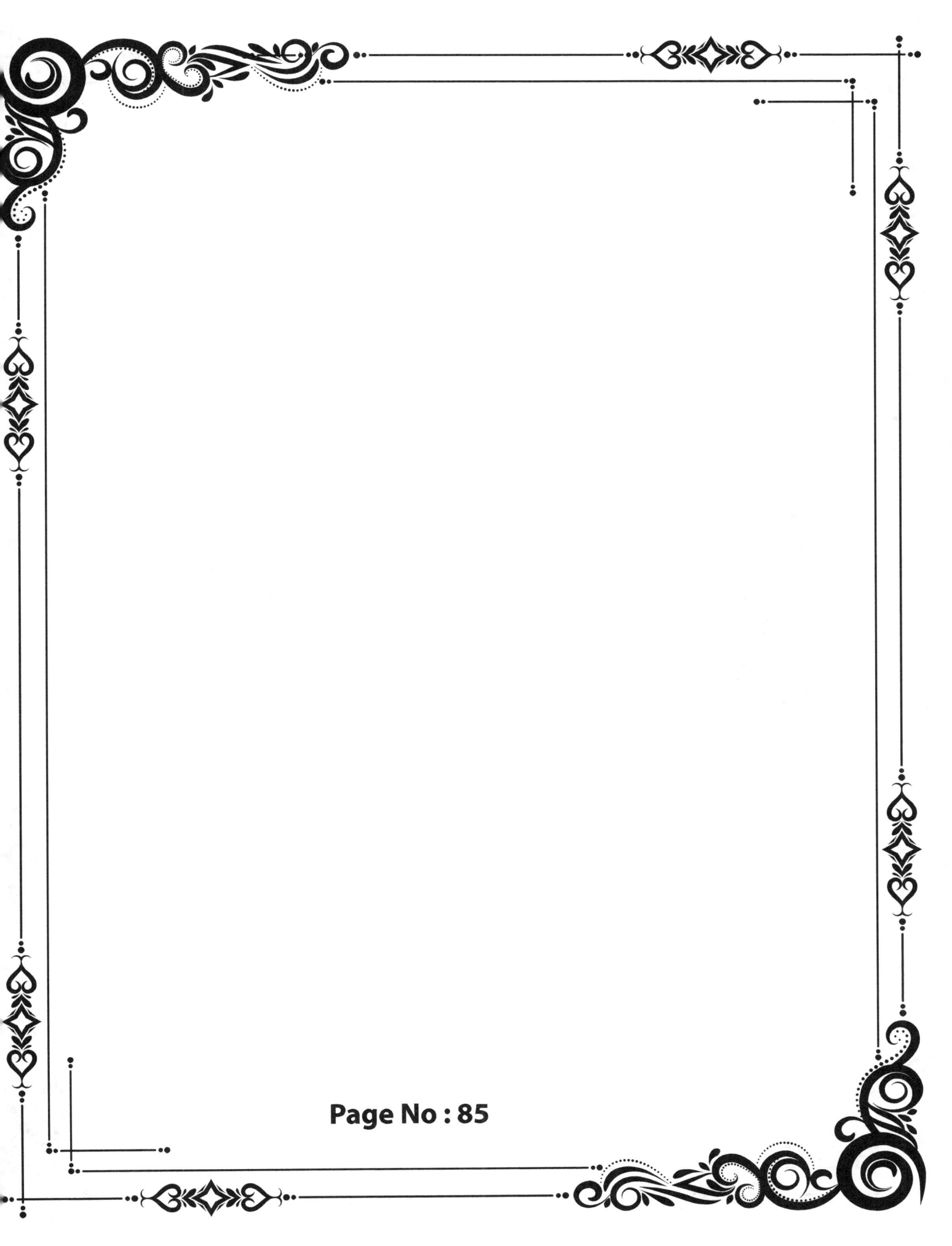

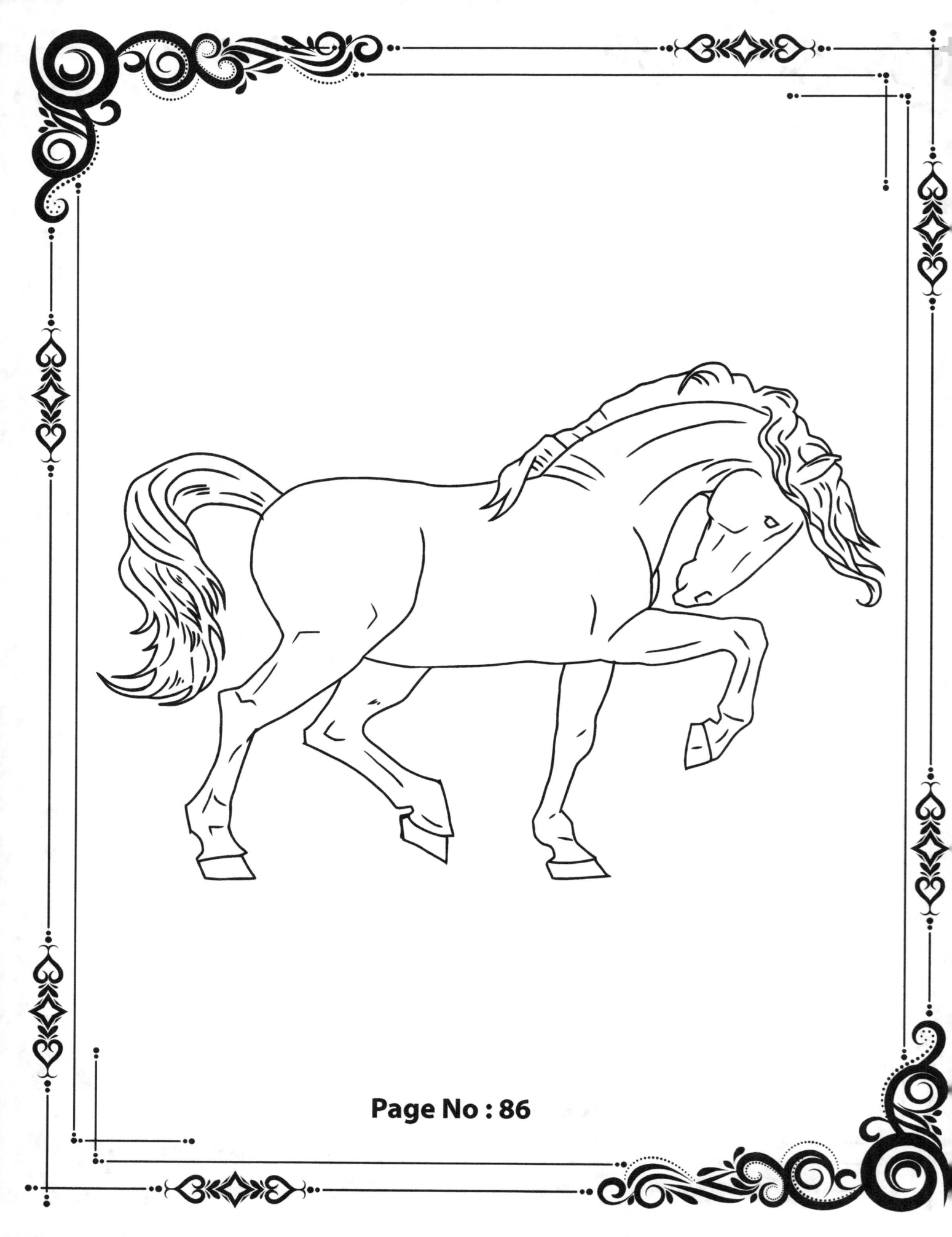

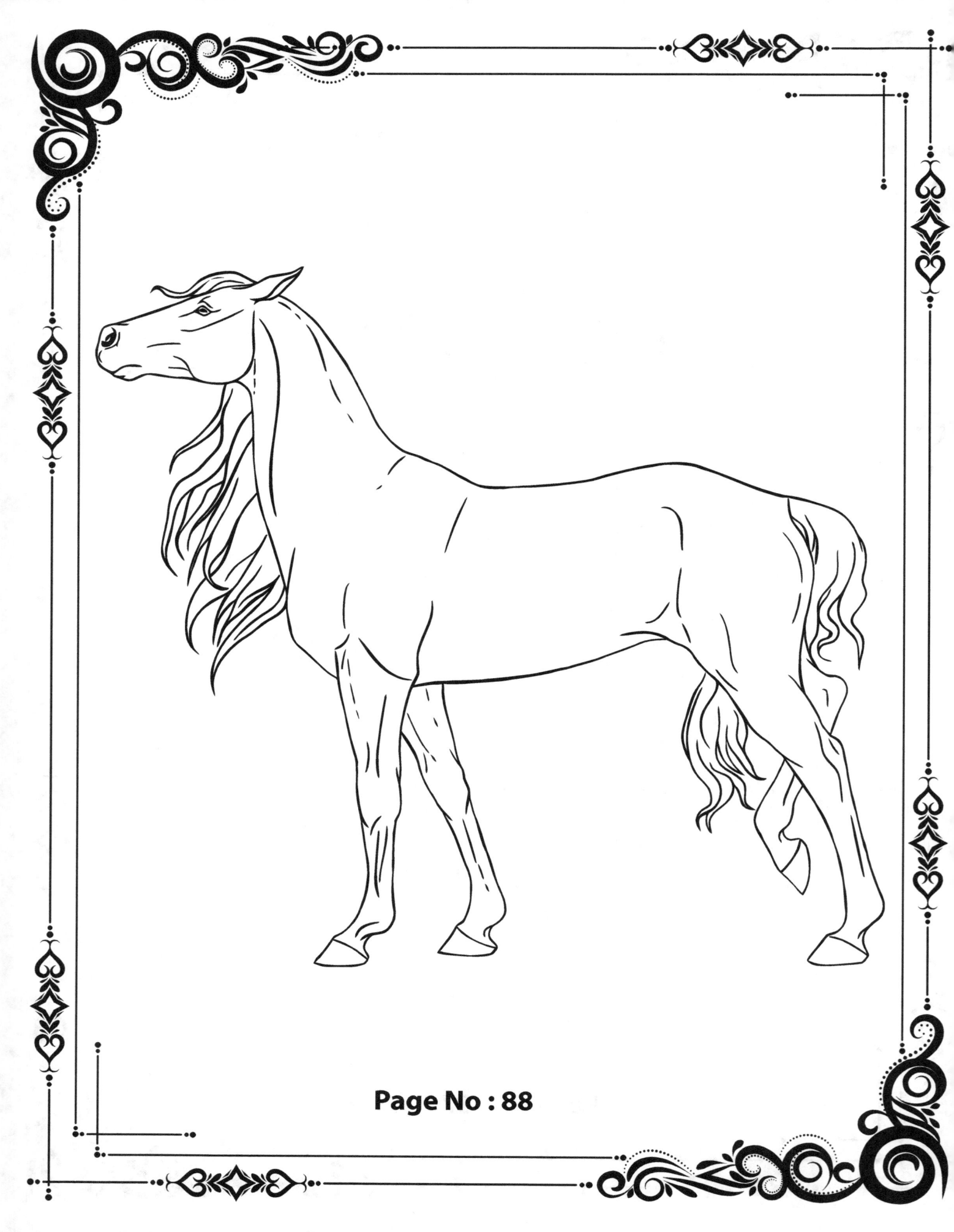

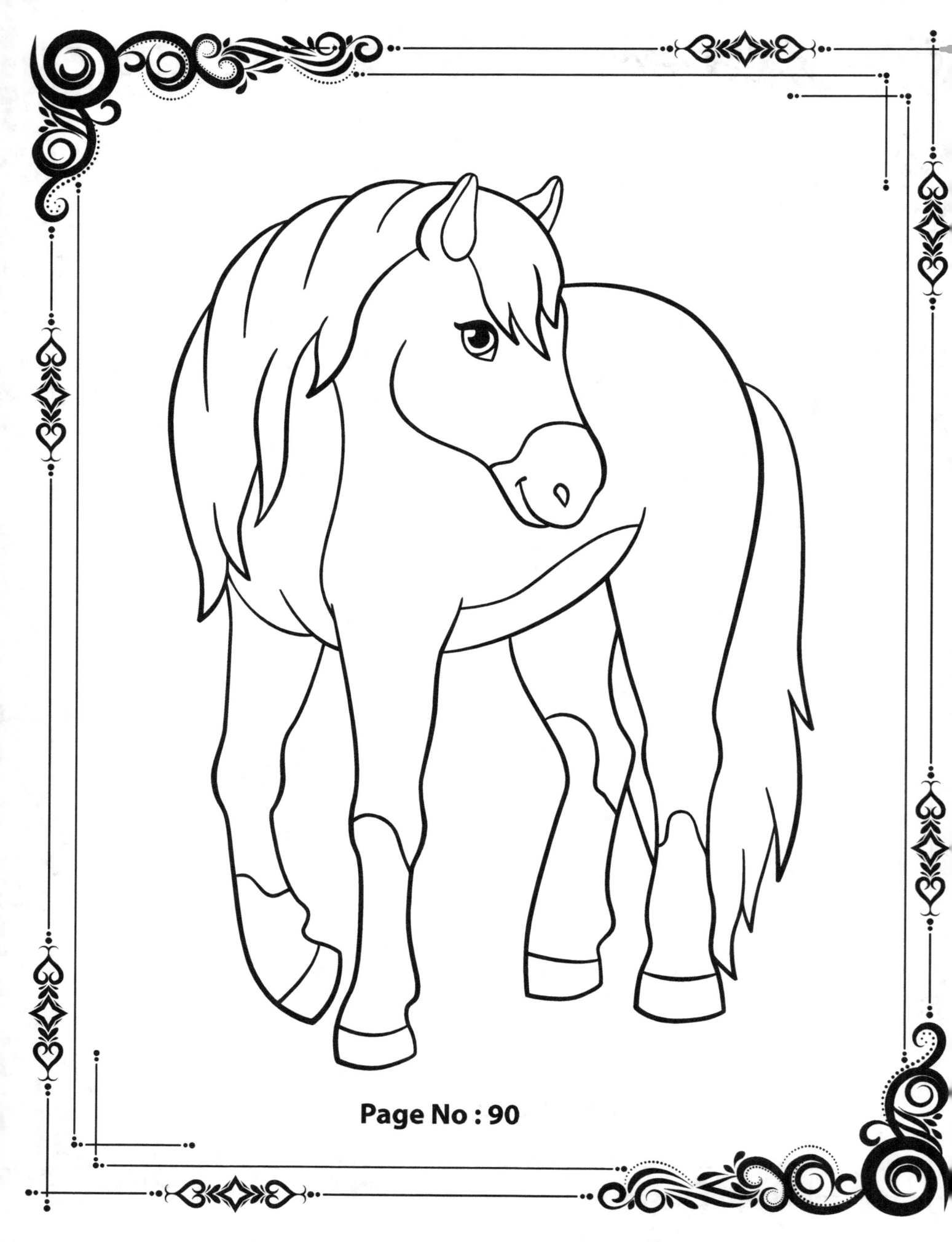

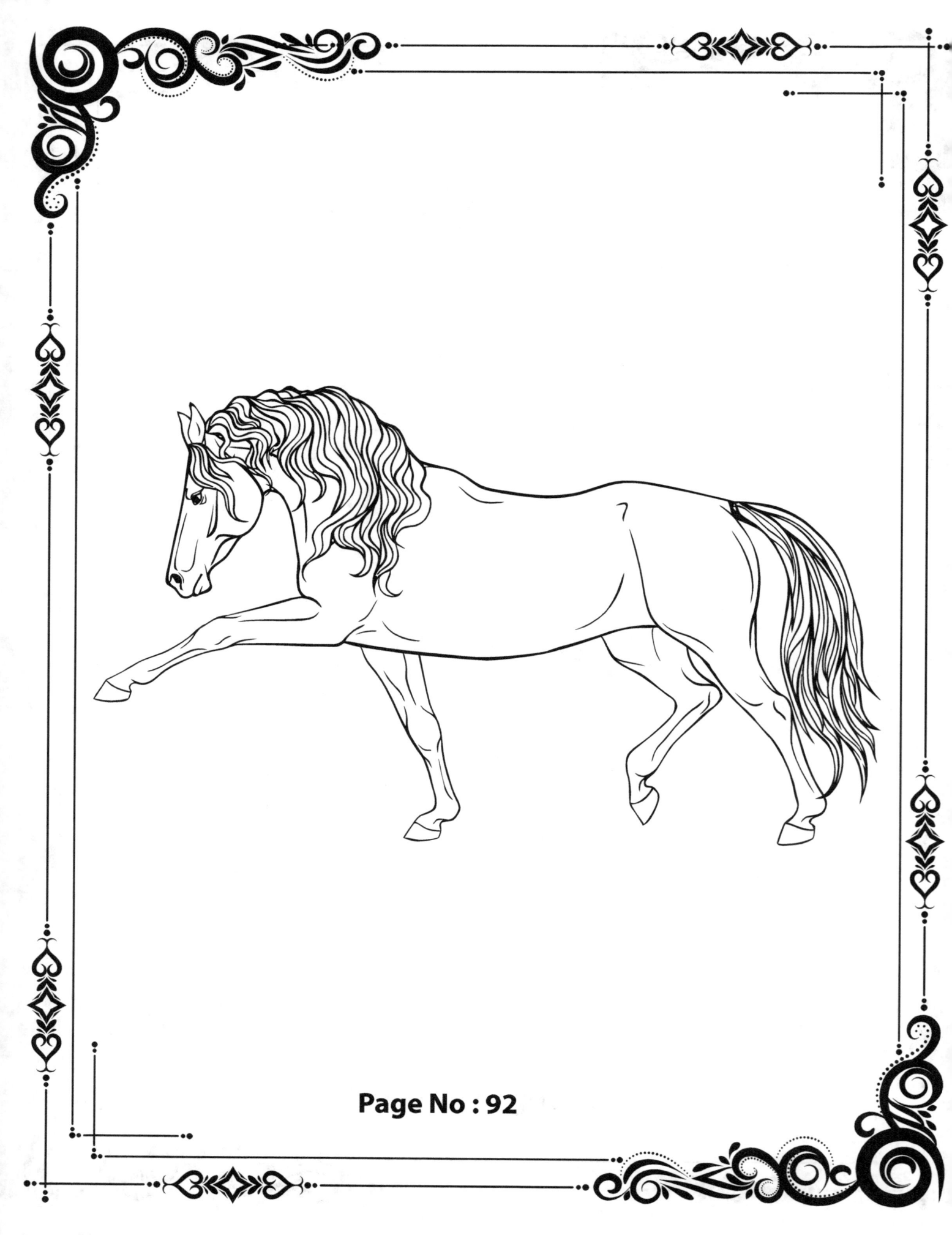

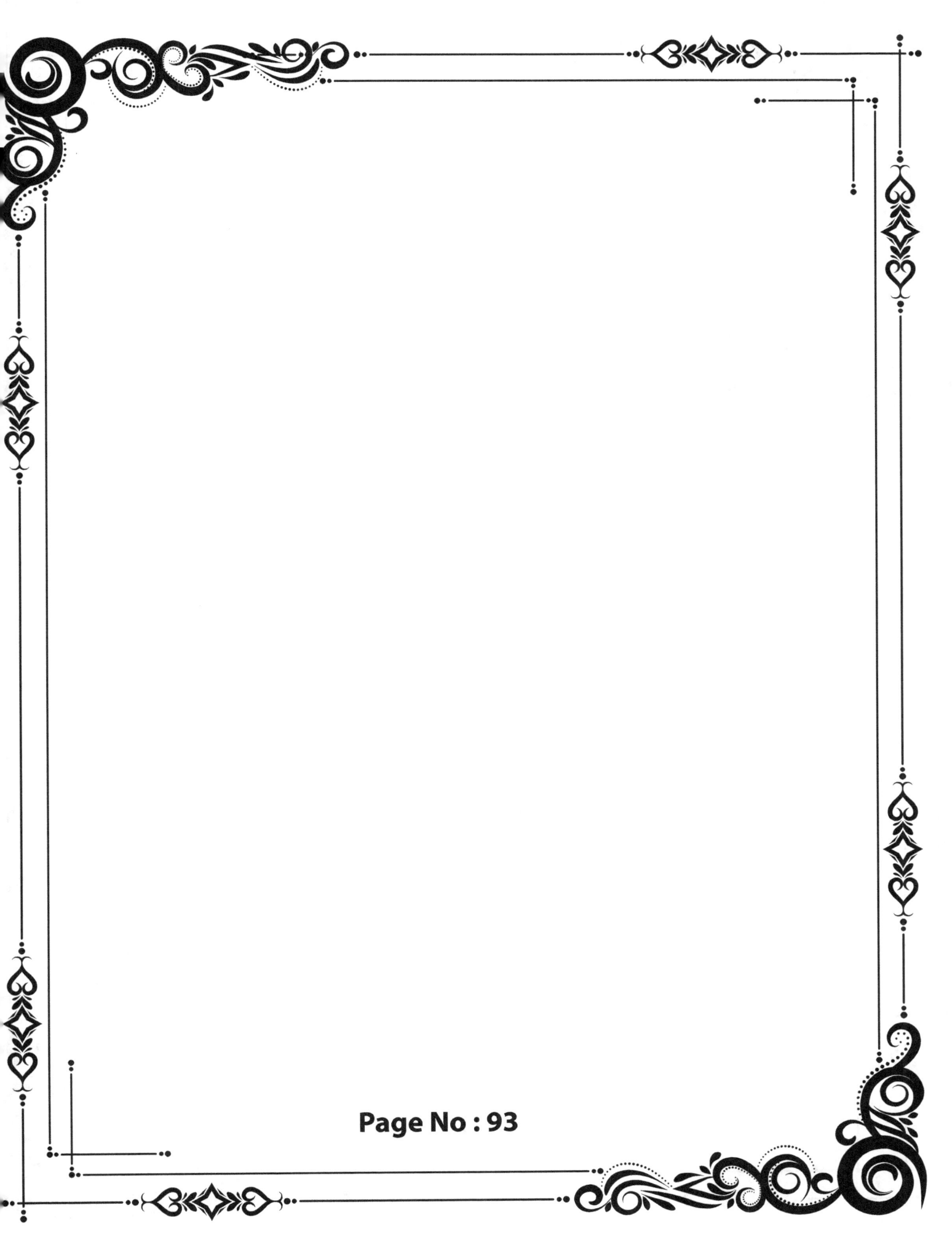

Page No : 93

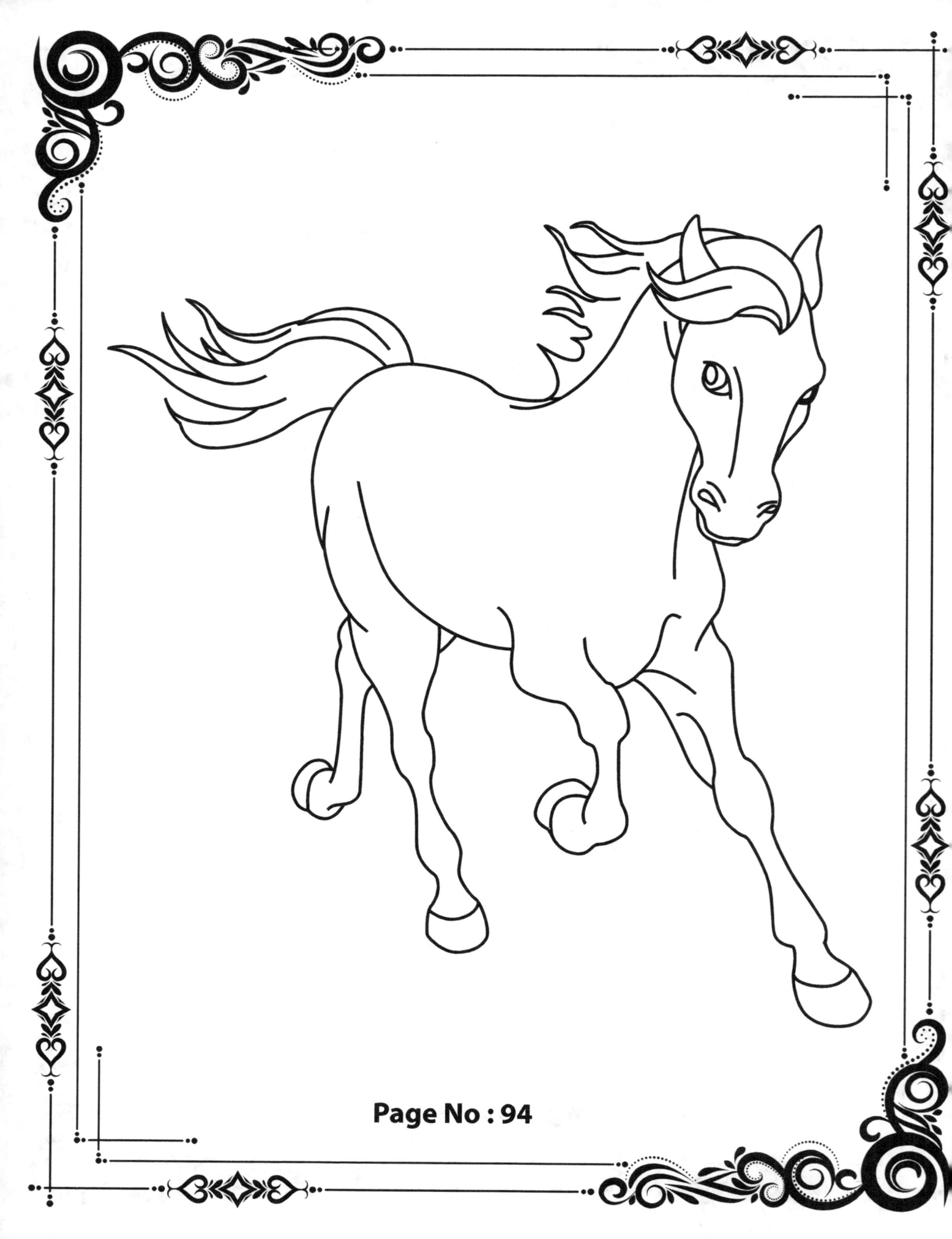

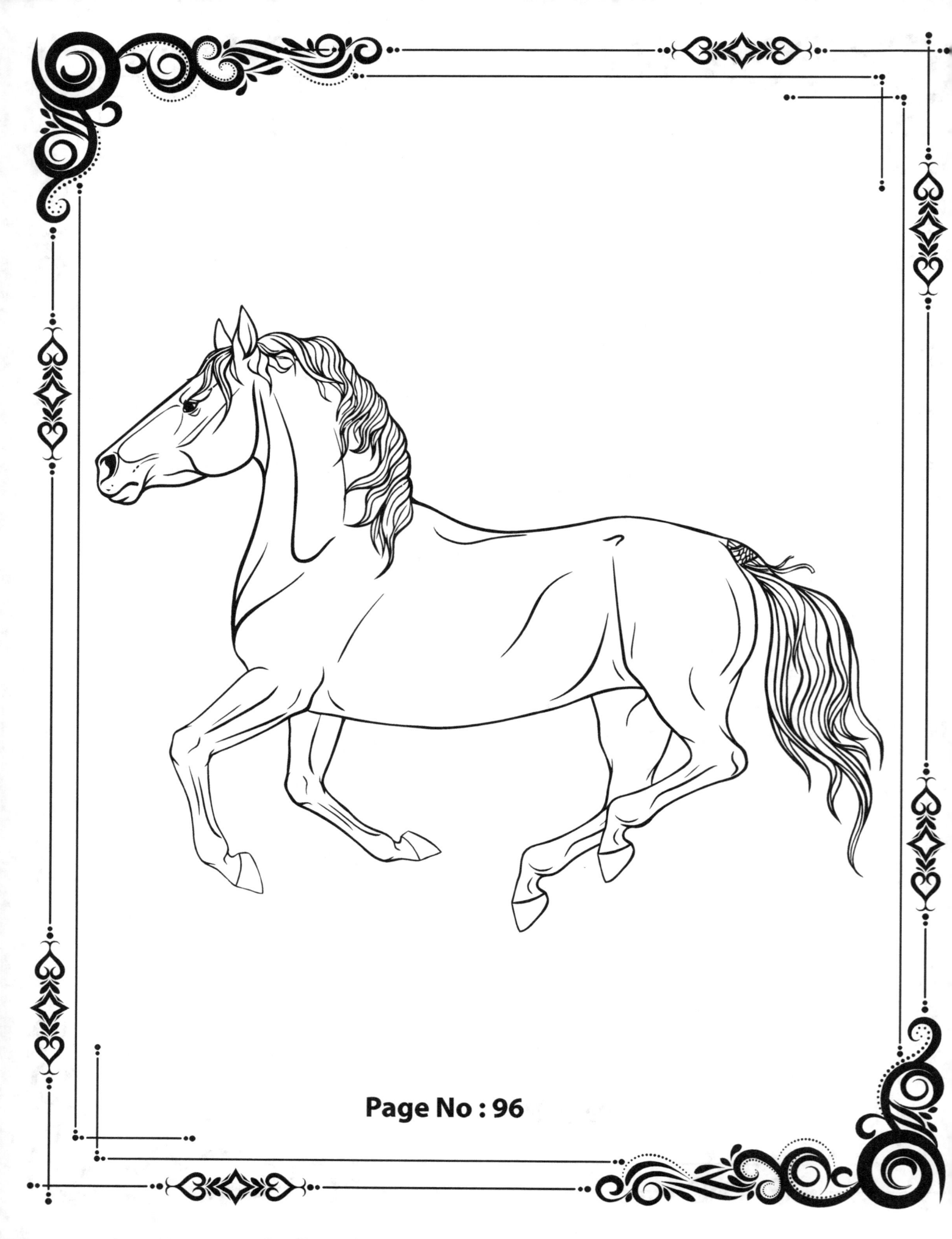

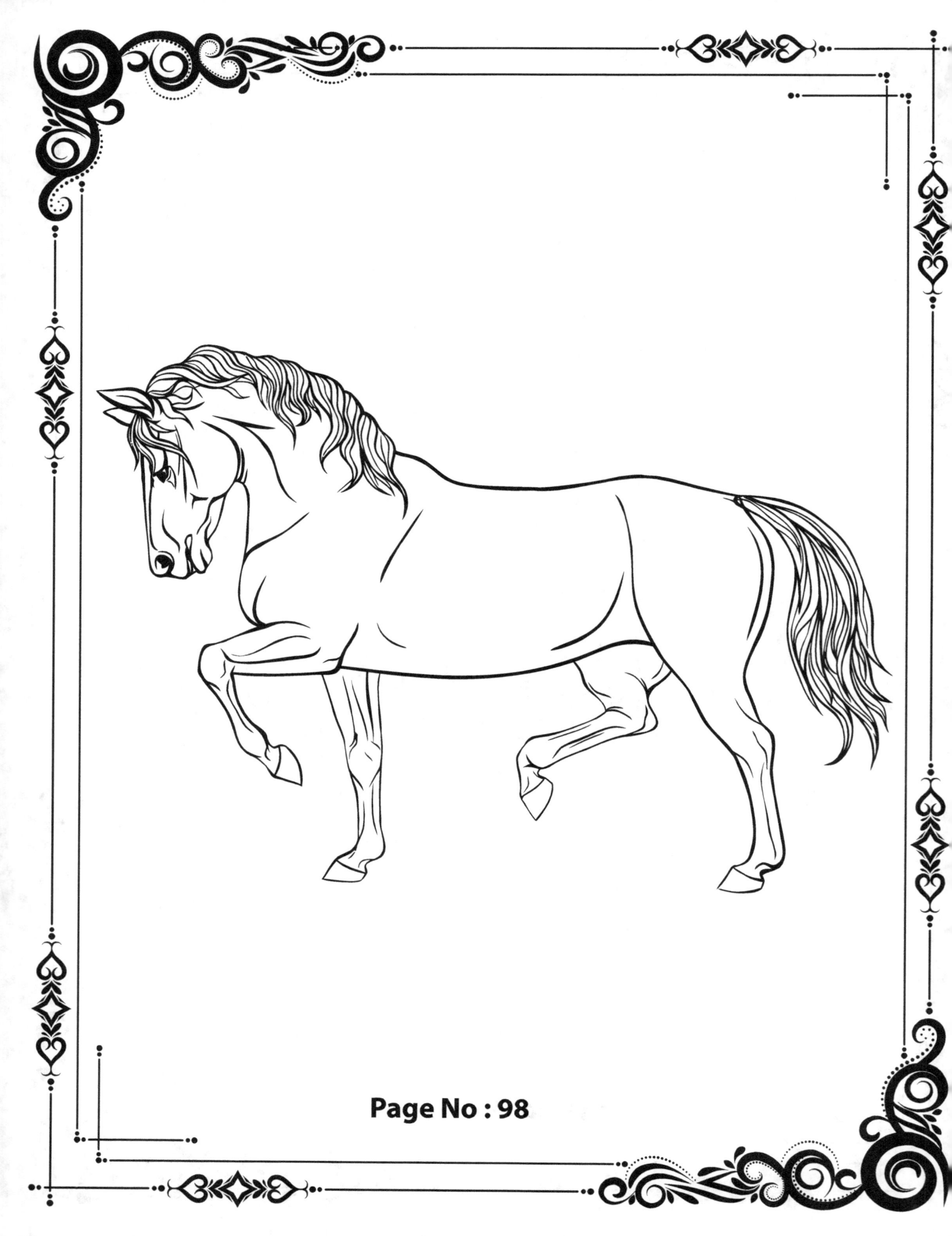

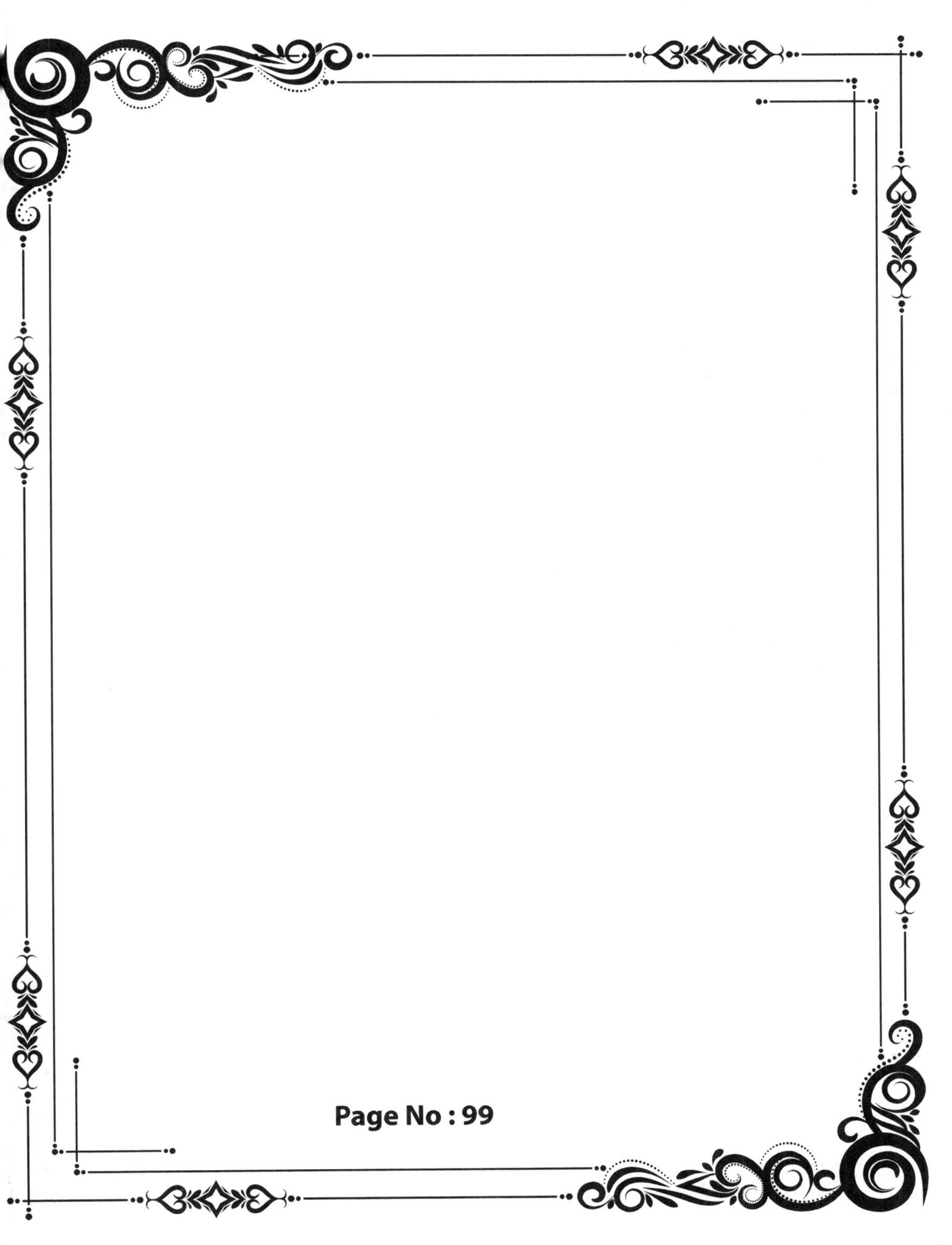

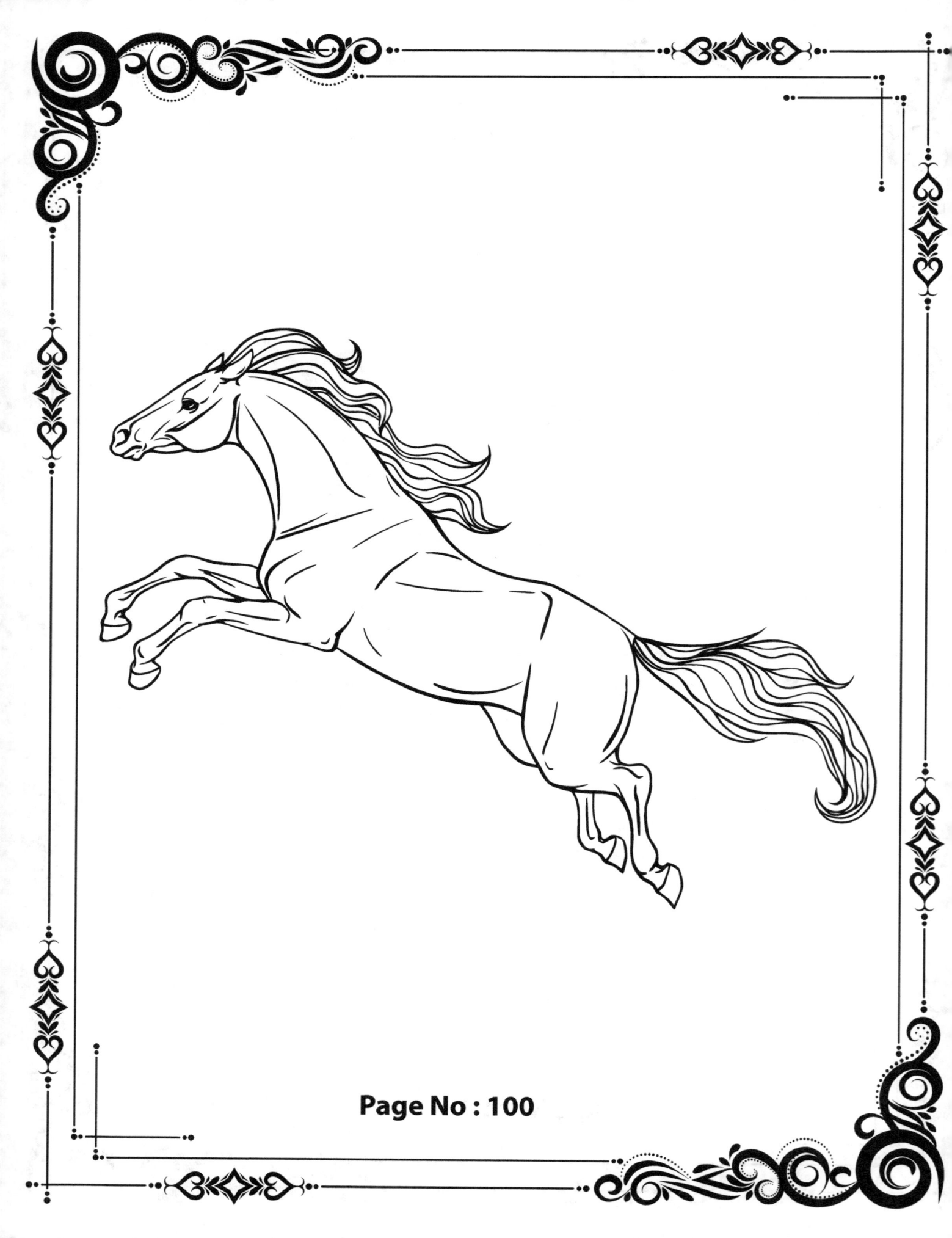

**Page No : 100**

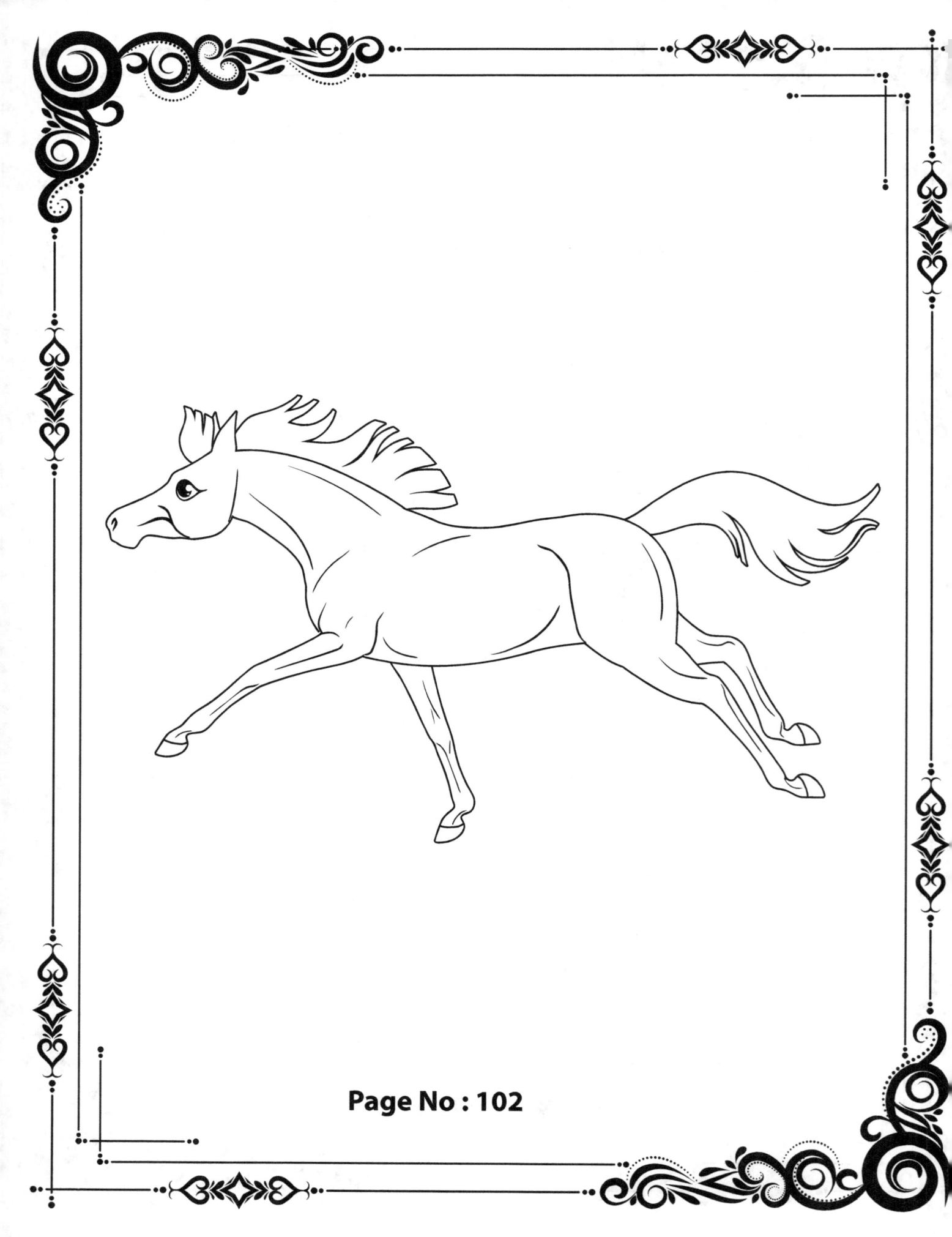

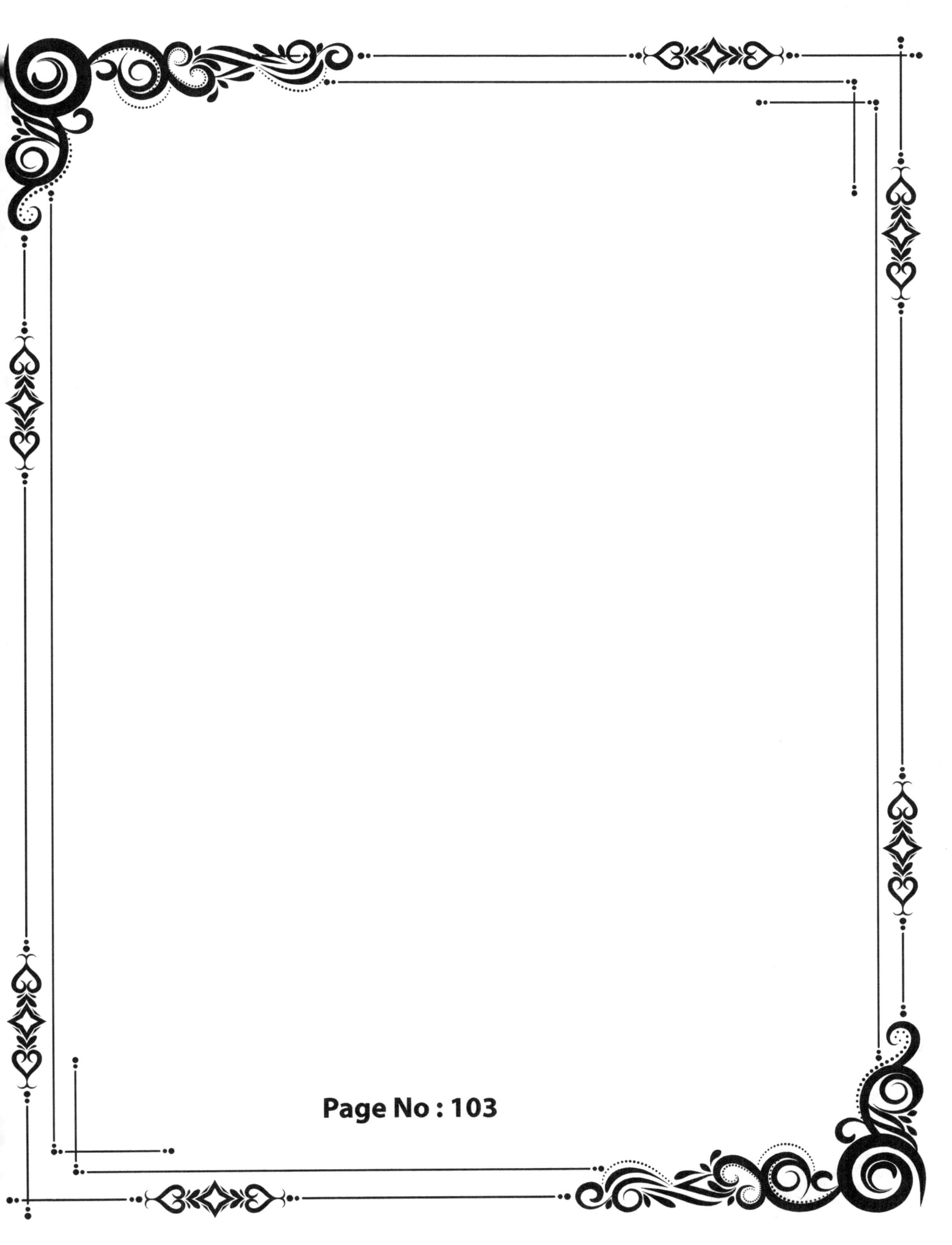

www.ingramcontent.com/pod-product-compliance
Lightning Source LLC
Chambersburg PA
CBHW081302170526
45165CB00011B/3378